homefront
insideout

To Sean and Paul Cunningham—who translate all our designs into reality

homefront

Inspirational ideas for your
home and garden from the
BBC TV series

insideout

Laurence Llewelyn-Bowen and Diarmuid Gavin

EXTERIORSCAPES, LLC
P.O. BOX 33711
SEATTLE, WA 98133

CONTENTS

introduction
GETTING TO GRIPS
WITH THE BASICS

above House or garden first? The house can provide a retreat from the bare patch outside, but it's difficult to avoid the garden for long if your room overlooks it.

Whenever we're working on a project, the same sort of conversations happen between ourselves and the client, and the same issues get discussed. So we thought it might be useful to commit a few of our answers and thoughts to paper, in the hope that at least some of the information might be helpful to you as you start out on your own design journey. And if you don't like our answers, then perhaps they might give you a starting point for your own ideas. So here goes.

House or garden first?
Laurence: I'd start with the garden.
There is nothing worse than looking out of the window on to the bare ground outside when the house is also in disarray with all the work going on inside.
Diarmuid: I'd start with the house. The garden can be a refuge from the interior work, but it's not practical to plan a garden without living with it first and seeing where the light falls over the day, the weeks, the months and the year.
Garden design is much more restricted than interior design by where the sun is; it is a practical constraint that needs to be addressed before you can decide where you want your patio or your plants to go. It is much more difficult to design the garden without this knowledge because most gardens are too small to work on in sections, whereas it's much easier to decorate a house gradually, room by room.

right Design is all about choosing a style that suits you – don't be afraid to move beyond traditional colours and materials.

far right Here the interior and exterior are working in harmony, with the living room directing the eye out through the glass doors to the patio beyond.

Where do you start with a design?

Laurence: Designing interiors is much more straightforward than designing exteriors because, unless you are wealthy enough to have 500 rooms, you will pretty much know what each room will be used for, and where to put the kids. For most of us the function of the various rooms is immediately obvious since your house will have been designed by an architect to have a kitchen, two reception rooms, etc.

You should, however, work out how you are going to use each room before you change the layout or structure of the house. It also helps to do a furniture plan – if you stick sheets of newspaper together to the appropriate size of your sofa, it will give you a good idea of how much space the furniture will fill. Once you've done this, you may find that it's better to make an opening in a wall rather than knock the whole thing out, so that you still have some space for shelves, or wall cupboards.

Diarmuid: Think about what you want to use the garden for – you will be trying to accommodate the needs of a variety of people and functions in one space; it requires careful planning to design a garden that is both practical and aesthetically pleasing. First, work out the pattern of the sun in your garden. It's an important part of planning your design. Most gardens will include some sort of seating area or patio, so you need to consider when you want to use the area before you decide where to put it. If you want to spend most time in your garden in the evenings after work, you'll probably want to put the patio where it will catch the last rays of the sun, or if you want to sit out during the day, you would

probably prefer a place in continuous sunlight. If entertaining is a major part of the garden's brief, you may decide that convenience is more important than sun and decide to put your patio area right next to your kitchen. It's up to you – the garden is your personal space and the most important thing to remember is that it should address your needs and desires.

Open-plan living

Diarmuid: I'm a great fan of open-plan living and space.

Laurence: Yes, but that's because you don't have children. Sometimes open-plan living can be too open; a vast amount of noise can be generated in an open-plan space. Even having a fairly restrained dinner party can disturb children sleeping upstairs. Openings are a good compromise because they give a sense of space without opening the room completely; this is something I've done in a few locations, particularly when creating one kitchen and dining room out of two rooms. Interiors are personal private space – do what you want, but don't forget that changes might have structural implications or be subject to planning restrictions.

far left With a huge array of materials now available, investigate your options thoroughly before you settle on your design style.

left Be creative with traditional features; functional need not always mean dull.

Tearsheets

Diarmuid: You should definitely use them. Sometimes you might have only a vague idea of how you want your garden to look and tearsheets are a brilliant way of focusing your ideas – even if they only help you decide what you don't want.

Laurence: Tearsheets have two jobs – to help you decide which flooring or furniture you like and what goes together, and they also help you discover how you want to feel in the space – tranquil, energetic or sociable, for example. It is a fantastic process. Tearsheets are invaluable and, ideally, every person in the house should produce their own. Surprisingly, you will often find that much of what each member of the family does and doesn't want or like will be quite similar, even if you haven't already discussed it.

Using magazines

Diarmuid: Looking through magazines can save you money and time. It is all too easy to buy a plant that you end up disliking when it's in your garden if you don't know what it will look like at maturity – how tall and wide it gets, or what its habit of growth will be. You would seldom do that within the house, because you usually know immediately whether or not you like a piece of furniture, a vase or whatever. Magazines can show you different plants and what they will look like at various stages of growth, and so can give you an idea of what size

they'll grow to, how much space they'll take up; they might even suggest companion plants that you would like.

Laurence: Magazines help you work out what you want so that you don't waft around; it's a way of forcing yourself to commit, because you are seeing a range of options. Builders say to me now that they love seeing tearsheets because it helps them to understand what the clients want and gives a very clear idea of what they are being asked to do.

Diarmuid: Use magazines to give you ideas, but don't be swayed by current trends. Garden plants and furniture remained more or less the same until the mid-1990s, but now you can buy so much more. Painting fences an insipid blue is a bad idea and there is no excuse. Don't do it just because you've seen it on TV or in a magazine, or because it's modern and contemporary – do it because you really like it.

Laurence: At least you can repaint a fence; large structures are a little more difficult to remove.

Linking the inside and outside of your house

Diarmuid: When Laurence and I work together, we don't discuss our plans, but the echoes in our designs are usually very striking. Often, our designs work better together when we design separately; other times, of course, he's just wrong.

Laurence: The common perception is that it's good to have a relationship between finishes inside and out, but this can often

right Experiment with shapes and designs; furniture should serve both an aesthetic and practical purpose in your schemes.

above A disused fireplace need not be a sad, empty space and an eyesore. With clever framing and styling it can become an interesting focal point instead.

appear too contrived. If you are building your house and garden from scratch it can work well, but it is a very different situation if you live in an established house and garden in the suburbs.

Diarmuid: Contrast can actually work much better than trying to match materials to create a link. In one design (p111), Laurence used dark blue tiles in his glass room, which jutted into the garden, and I used pale stone paving on the patio outside the windows. In that case the contrast worked really well, but it also made a link between the interior and the garden.

Remember to create the space to give a clear view of the garden from the house. Don't allow clutter or a wall of plants outside the doors or window, to obscure your view of the garden, and don't block exits with furniture on the inside or on the outside.

Laurence: It is rare for an interior to have an impact on the garden, so you don't usually need to take into consideration how it will look from outside. You may not like the view from outside, because it may be the architecture of the house that you don't like, but it is difficult to change this and most houses in the UK don't suit the tweaking of their exterior style.

Diarmuid: If you really hate the exterior of your house, you can plant up the walls with attractive climbers to soften or partially mask unsightly architecture.

Laurence: Front gardens can enhance the appearance of your house. They can be statements and often reflect a very British attitude – concealing personal taste by having a house that is conventional on the outside, but modern and sexy on the inside.

Diarmuid: A front garden may be conventional because it is public, but the back garden is a private space where people feel they can go mad.

Explore the boundaries of design

Laurence: Your design should be down to your own personal taste – the concept of good and bad taste no longer has any credibility.

Diarmuid: Our schemes are for people to react to, rather than to copy. They are the ultimate of what the garden can be, for people to take ideas and inspiration from, but not to mimic slavishly. People might react against some of my designs and instead feel they prove that the simplicity of an English country garden is more beautiful than a contemporary design.

Laurence: By reacting against a scheme you decide on your style. People are more intelligent about design now, they won't dismiss a scheme outright; instead they will select and use elements from it that they like.

above Using natural materials such as stone and wood can create a tranquil environment away from the chaos of the modern world.

above But hot pinks and outdoor fires can create a Mediterranean atmosphere for those who see the garden as a place for entertaining.

Diarmuid: By using planting, colour, contemporary materials, and containers in grand designs you stimulate people's imaginations, and we often find that elements of the designs will filter down into gardens in a smaller, perhaps more practical way.

Laurence: *Home Front* is a sort of catwalk collection, with *haute couture* designs. As in the fashion world, it is up to the retailers to take these ideas and filter them down to consumers in a more readily available form. People today crave simplicity and comfort in their homes; there has been a slowdown in contemporary design recently, because people are more confident about bringing what they like into a design.

Most housing in this country tends to be quite modern and often has very little character, but this can work in your favour as these houses are ideally suited to bringing in features such as fireplaces, regardless of the period in which it was built.

Diarmuid: Don't be afraid to design the kind of garden that you really want, even if it isn't in keeping with the period of your house. Very contemporary styles can blend with classical and traditional designs extremely well, don't feel you have to restrict yourself simply to one or the other; you can bring in both. Have your cake and eat it.

Don't forget...

Laurence: Be personal – work hard to find something that you like and use your research to push out the boundaries of what you know.

Diarmuid: Give yourself time. We're so influenced by today's pace and by doing things quickly. Stop and listen to your garden and to what it is saying to you. There is no point in being inspired and not being able to justify it.

Laurence: Patience is important – give yourself a year to understand the way the sun comes into the garden or house, and make decisions based on these observations. People are staying in their homes longer, so separate out the quick-fix solutions from the longer-term solutions.

left In today's society we all seem to crave privacy in the garden. This wall addresses the issue, creating a room away from the rest of the garden. But this circular opening in the wall prevents the space from feeling too enclosed.

below As solid structures, high walls have the disadvantage of blocking out light into your plot. Using tall plants instead, such as this bamboo, can provide a screen whilst still allowing light through.

Designing on a budget

Laurence: It is very hard to do a professional, accountable job when trying to do innovative things, particularly on the programme when we are always battling against time.

Diarmuid: Try to budget your plan as best you can, but don't get stressed if it goes awry. It almost always goes wrong somewhere along the line and you will often run out of money halfway through a job. That's the reason that it's so often recommended that you phase the work to suit your budget.

Laurence: If you are exceeding your budget, or think you're about to, keep a copy of your tearsheet handy so you can keep in your mind what the finished design will be like. It will give you faith to go on with it, either now, or later, when funds are a bit more healthy.

Privacy

Diarmuid: Why do we always want to avoid our neighbours? Don't we want to get to know them? There is a need today for people to have their own personal, private space at times, and this is where an outdoor room can be the perfect solution. But if you do want to screen the whole garden, screen the area sensitively – don't plant massive hedges that could cause problems in your garden or with your neighbours. Choose tall plants or trees with foliage that will let some light through. You might want to keep out prying eyes, but you don't want to block out all your sunlight in the process.

Laurence: People do want to create their own private haven, to retreat to cocoons where they can be themselves. It is a sign of a society under pressure when it has become so much more important for people to have privacy and a sanctuary from the world. People have a tremendous need for a regression to a more peaceful state when they get home from work and a desire to escape from angst-creating technology. Don't come home and draw all the curtains though, nets may be out of style, but sheer curtains are very much in vogue and will give you some privacy without giving the room an oppressive sense of enclosure.

left Garden lighting no longer has to serve a purely practical purpose; instead it can add drama and entertainment to your scheme.

simpler way of living. There is also a huge range of lighting that is better suited to a more energetic or party atmosphere.

Think about the mood you want to create when you decide on your lighting scheme. Remember to arrange your lights carefully to get the effect you want – sometimes illuminating random features with spot lights can create the unfortunate impression of a dodgy hotel.

Diarmuid: People are more sophisticated in their tastes now and manufacturers are responding to their needs, but there is still a lot of bad stuff around on the market – unsubtle lighting and plastic sofas that are both uncomfortable and ugly. Some manufacturers' ideas are still bound-up with the needs of interior design, and they are adapting them to the garden. What is actually needed is that designs for garden accessories originate from within the garden, so that form follows function. Slowly, some companies are beginning to grasp the difference.

Laurence: Manufacturers do need to break away from the interior traditions, as designing for the garden should be a separate discipline. The popularity of decking proves that people are confident with moving outdoors, but they need more confidence with planting.

Diarmuid: The big problem is that, after a sort of design stasis for so many years, there has been a blind rush

Lighting and technology

Diarmuid: Technology in the garden is becoming more important now as people want to prolong their time outside. Having been at work all day, people want to get home and see their garden in the evenings and spend time in it. Lighting and patio heaters mean that the garden can now be a place you can sit in beyond the few short high-summer months.

As well as having practical functions, lighting can be used for entertainment effects, for evenings when the garden becomes a place to party, or to spend time with friends. Coloured lighting and fibre-optic lights in walls and flooring can have a wonderfully dramatic effect. And as we use the garden now as an extension of our interiors, power points in the garden mean that it can be a place to listen to music, watch television or work on your laptop.

Laurence: Inside and outside, the simplest forms of lighting can often be the best – candles and lamps have a wonderfully soothing effect and reflect a desire for a

left and above A garden needn't be just a place you visit in the summer – with a little planning and imagination, it can be an exciting or therapeutic space all year round.

forward in garden design that has led to some ridiculous concepts.

However, the great joy is that more people are using gardens than ever before, and although there have been fewer innovations in the garden than in interiors, that is now starting to change, and the whole family is getting involved in gardening, rather than people turning to it in middle age.

Laurence: People will bring the same sophistication to the garden as they do inside. There is a softening happening in interior design at the moment that will hit gardens soon and then we'll have simplicity in design throughout home and garden.

Enjoy your garden

Diarmuid: Today people want a simple life after work and don't have the time to maintain complicated plots. I am most often asked to design low-maintenance plots for people who love plants and the idea of a garden, but just don't have the time to do a lot of gardening. But I do find that people get hooked once they get into it – they want to look after their plants as they do their cats.

People are amazed at what plants do, and then they want to nurture them and get tips on gardening.

Laurence: People ought to enjoy gardening and get pleasure from it. Most of us don't feel we have much that is spiritual in our lives, but gardening is an intensely spiritual experience.

Diarmuid: Gardening can be a very therapeutic as well as creative exercise. We see old photographs of people dressed up for gardening, but now we garden for pleasure to grow plants and vegetables, not just to tend the lawn and dead-head roses.

Laurence: Gardening was once a social statement. But it has moved on and we feel reassured that nature exists when we leave the technology in the office and head home. We are not decorating our homes or gardens now to keep up with the Joneses, or to make things look pretty, it has become a very personal pleasure. Interior and exterior design are undergoing the most fantastic advances that keep pace with other social advances – they celebrate our diverse society and individuality – our own and the ability to recognize other people's. It's a very exciting time.

inside
INTERIOR DESIGN

insideout
AN INTRODUCTION TO INTERIOR DESIGN

INTERIOR DESIGN THEN AND NOW

As a nation, our attitude to design has changed immeasurably over the past few years. There are several closely related reasons for this, but they all spring from the same root – the creation of an individual, personal cocoon as an antidote to the stresses of daily living. For previous generations – in fact, speaking frankly, for most of us ten years ago – the way the home looked was about very different things. We decorated to fit in, we decorated to keep up with the Joneses, we decorated in the way our parents decorated because change was scary, or we decorated to impress.

Looking back, it's easy to sneer but, to be fair, the presentation of a room had, for centuries, been conceived to meet one, or indeed all of those criteria. To a large extent, the look of our rooms was beyond our control; the look of our rooms was a statement – easily read by peers, superiors or, indeed, inferiors alike – that defined where we fitted in to the dreaded British class system. Anyone with ideas (for ideas read 'Taste') above their station was shot down in flames as a pretentious nouveau artiste. But then, quite suddenly, something changed.

Normally, change in design was led by the dictates of powerful taste gurus who pronounced, expecting the country to follow, that 'black was the new black', or that rococo was out and neo-classical was in. Design moved seamlessly overnight from an autocracy to a democracy and the bloodless revolution was effected by us, the people.

Economics played an important role; the increase in home ownership, a steadily growing economy, the almost total assimilation of women into the workplace, the ubiquitous expansion of the middle classes and, of course, the fact that

right For many of us, simplicity is an important rallying cry. Here a display niche contains two carefully considered, edited objects.

far right Even in the 21st century, with all the technological advances in heating and lighting, at home we're still drawn to real flame like proverbial moths.

you and I, by and large, had more disposable cash in our pockets. Coupled with this, there were more and more easily digestible ways of finding out about design.

The steadily ascending plume of magazines suddenly became a mushroom cloud of interiors information, and design became a mainstay of prime time television schedules. This gave us all access to more than enough examples of how to decorate a room, which inevitably encouraged all of us to explore and define what our personal, individual tastes were. Retailers being retailers, product ranges offered in the shops went from desultory to omnifarious within months, and the high street became a brightly coloured miasma of decorating do-dahs.

Now, as if all that wasn't a heady enough cocktail, a new and far more powerful element hit the mix. To fund our newly glamorous lifestyles, to pay for the holidays, meals out and refurbishment campaigns, we needed money – for which we had to work, and the harder we worked the more we got. Simple, but, of course, the inevitable downside of all work and minimal playtime began to hit home.

We became a 'stressed, time-poor' nation (an expression borrowed from our American cousins): zombies constantly under the thumb of our bosses and our responsibilities, with the technology that dominates our workplaces constantly reminding us how clever it is and, by comparison, how stupid we are. We needed a retreat, a cocoon, an oasis where wounds could be licked and batteries recharged. The home… it's not really such a new concept; societies under stress are always prone to idealize the hearth and home.

Your home is your personal space, somewhere where you, and you alone, have total personal control. For most people, being in charge of how the living room looks is one of the few areas of purely personal responsibility in their lives. So where has that left us as a nation? Nervy clock-watchers constantly daydreaming of being at home? Not necessarily: but if not, then principally, I believe, because we've learnt to decorate so well. These days, our homes are deeply personal, deeply expressive statements of individuality. Who would have thought that the colour of your dining room would say so much about you?

PLANNING YOUR DESIGN

Before diving headfirst into design, it is essential to establish, and then stick to, your own parameters. Cost is usually one of the first limits one has to set; use is also an obviously important point to define. Incorporating the needs of all those likely to use the space takes consideration; as does, at the most basic level, anything in the room you need to work around. It's a rare but happy moment when a design scheme can be considered that does not need to work around an existing piece of furniture, recently installed expensive floor covering, or highly prized family heirloom of some description.

Design is at its most fulfilling when all of the constraints placed upon the project are considered and accommodated, and yet the trial scheme remains a powerful, personal statement. It's difficult for us to divorce ourselves from the good, solid British tradition of design established by the designers of, say, the Arts and

Crafts movement, like William Morris in the 19th century. And why should we? He passionately believed that very old truth that design should create a fusion between beauty and usefulness, aesthetics and practicality.

At the end of the day, a design has to work, but working out what you want is not easy. On the programme, we often use the clients' tearsheet as a device to help them communicate the direction they want to take. These have been a real innovation; they insist that the client sits down and tries to reconcile the look they have in their minds with the visual imagery taken from magazines. It produces a crazy collage of finishes, pictures, colours and motifs, but never underestimate the power of the tearsheet, for it can reveal much more than just a favourite colour. The successful tearsheet presentation should not only give you a jolly good stab at assessing how you want a space to look, but should also project how you would like to feel when occupying it.

Having frightened you with the psychological power of the tearsheet, let me just ram home its more prosaic, but nevertheless equally important function. Unlike those on *Home Front,* most refurbishments do not fly by in three weeks; they drag on and on as projects are completed bit by bit to keep pace with finances, or the whim of your builder. In your case, it's essential that you

have a record of the scheme as a whole. Sitting in a room with painted walls and new floor, but no curtains or sofa, can weaken the resolve of even the most steadfast home improver. If, on the other hand, you have in front of you a picture of the remaining elements, you'll find it much easier to take heart.

As any professional designer will tell you, lists run the planet. Interior design requires list after list after list. For your builder/decorator/plumber/electrician to understand what you want, you'll need to give them a list. To project how much the whole thing is going to cost, you'll need a list. To finalize what you will need in the room, you'll need a list. For list-o-phobes it sounds like hell but, speaking as a strictly anti-list human, I have to admit to quite enjoying them for interior design. Good organization is essential for you to ensure that the job gets done for the money you have to spend, in the time you have given for it to happen, and to ensure that the finished effect is achieved to your complete satisfaction.

Inspiration

Interior design inspiration can come from anywhere or anything. Obviously the majority of our interior schemes derive ultimately from an existing solution applied by someone else, but I'm a great believer in

above Hall stairs and landings suit dramatic effects since, as transitional areas, the experience is always quick.

above Lighting needn't just be a bulb on a flex; here neon shines through perspex.

casting the net of inspiration in as broad an arc as possible. Art, fashion, graphics, music, even – dare I say it – gardens, can throw up some surprisingly inspirational elements, each with the potential to trigger an original interior design solution.

The best architects and designers have always prided themselves on the depth and diversity of their knowledge and sources of inspiration. A designer like Charles Rennie Mackintosh knew all there was to know about the European architectural tradition up to his time, but he also went out of his way to study Japanese design, learning its elegant vocabulary backwards.

This depth of knowledge meant that when he sat down to design a scheme, the most incredible fusion of ideas and inspirations happened. Elements borrowed from a vast array of sources were reinterpreted in those highly personal, original combinations so characteristic of Mackintosh's instantly recognizable style.

So when seeking inspiration, cast your net wide, do your research well and enjoy every minute of it. Sitting in front of a blank sheet of paper, waiting for inspiration to strike is, for me, just a passionate fiction.

Light and colour

Colour is a very interesting, highly subjective issue. As I have said, we have now grown up to the personal possibilities of the way our homes look, and, so often, this individuality is most efficiently expressed in the colours we choose.

I believe people feel an instinctive draw to particular ends of the chromatic scale. One person might find themselves consistently falling in love with oranges, reds and yellows, while their neighbour finds hot colours anathema, choosing only cool blues or greens to express their personal taste. There is yet another section of the colour-consuming public who operate in the space

left Traditional needn't mean dull. In fact, historically-inspired decorating offers so many opportunities for jaw-dropping effects and clever interplays of colour.

right Colour can be one of the most important weapons in the interior design armoury. Even subtle, tonal schemes profit from an accent.

far right Modern design need not lack comfort, detail or interest. There are of course plenty of minimalists who would recoil in horror at the concept of a vase but the crucial point to remember is that your interior is for you alone.

below Never feel too busy to treat yourself to clever details – they are what will give you continued pleasure as you use the room.

between: purples, turquoises, aquas, cucumber greens – a subtle, shape-shifting lot who've discovered the secret of fusing cool and warm for a truly balanced effect.

One element in the colour choice procedure that few consider is the quality of light streaming through our windows. Around the Mediterranean, light floods into rooms with a cheeky, warm apricot glow. During the long, Scandinavian summer days, light in Swedish drawing rooms is clean, pure and chromatically balanced. In Britain, thanks to our temperate but largely overcast climate, light is frequently grey, often green-tinted by the time it's bounced off fields, trees or roadside grass verges.

You might also consider the direction that light comes from, and that its tone changes through the day. Compare the bright, fresh light of morning, for example, with the colour warmth that is more typical of evening light. A clever interior design scheme takes account of this and works with colour to compensate for smudgy illumination. Warmer colours or cooler, light-reflective ones can be used to rebalance the quality of light, nudging it ever so gently in a less chilly direction.

Practical issues

Always make sure that what you want to do in a room is going to fit. I know this sounds ridiculously obvious and rather nanny-esque advice, but I've seen far too many rooms where the 3-piece suite fits only with thanks to a shoe-horn, and the family's lack of cat is all to the good since there would be no room to swing one if they had one.

Making a simple sketch plan and marking out on it the size of furniture is clearly a helpful start. For anyone befuddled by the vagaries of scale, be more hands-on. Stick newspapers together to match the exact dimensions of each piece of furniture and then move them around the empty room until you feel that you have achieved a layout that is workable.

There are few areas of the home where practicality can be thrown out of the window, but practicality needn't mean a lack of creativity. Half the fun is making something improbably glam implausibly practical, but try to avoid silliness or faddishness. Unless, of course, you are deep down, dyed in the wool, silly enough or faddish enough not to notice how raggedy your room looks after a few weeks.

Being sensible about budget also helps. There's plenty that's cheap; there's plenty that's expensive nowadays but, by and large, our accepting, accommodating design democracy celebrates a mixture of the two, particularly when it comes to so-called fashion items. Our parents, bless them, decorated for life, pronouncing gloomily that 'this sofa will see me out', or 'these curtains have been up since I was thirty and, at seventy, I see little point in changing them'.

We very much rebelled against that standpoint and, a few years ago, were in danger of going too far the other way. Disposable, throw-away design crept dangerously but seductively through our front doors. I suppose we were like kids in a sweet shop, spoiled for choice, wanting everything regardless of the damage it might do to our teeth, or our pockets.

Nowadays, I'm happy to report that we're back on the rails, making intelligent decisions about how much we spend on date-sensitive, Day-Glo, fur-fabric cushions, or disco-inspired light fittings. If that's your taste, then fine, gather it to your bosom. But bear in mind that in design, as in so many other things, all that glitters is not gold. In fact, half the time, it actually is glitter.

So, it's a brave new design world in which anything goes as long as you really want it. Quality is celebrated and, even more importantly, it is valued over price. Remember that it's not how much you spend, it's how well you've spent it that counts.

Home Front will continue to celebrate the diversity that defines design today and, more than that, will continue to be your guide as it exposes the workings of the design procedure and, heaven forbid, the convolutions of the designer's mind. The one thing to remember is, if you want it, do it. Your home is your best friend, but more than this, it can be one of your most important allies in your battle against the stresses of life.

inside out
KITCHENS

above The reflective potential of metal has become a true friend in today's kitchen design.

THE KITCHEN THEN AND NOW

Over successive generations, the kitchen has been dragged up from servant-wing obscurity to become the heart of the home. Before the 1950s, the very idea of designing a kitchen was bizarre – it was a working environment where one employed people to wash, chop and prepare food. These days, of course, unless one has a machine to do all the above, one has to do it all for oneself. Thus was the modern kitchen born.

Help from the experts

For our generation, the kitchen is one area we are used to spending money on and, generally, we will employ a professional to design it. I feel strongly that kitchen design is a specific discipline with many practical and technical considerations, which is why, as an interior designer, I welcome the association with another professional. Employing a kitchen professional, or finding the right fitter, even soaking up the advice given in a store or in the magazines, helps enormously, and, indeed, is essential from a safety point of view, no matter how expert at DIY you are. Do as I do, remove the yoke of practicality – pass it on to someone who knows about the plumbing, electricity and so on. Focus instead on the atmosphere and the environment you wish to create.

Designing for your space

Space-saving cleverness is so often key to a successful, useful and good-looking kitchen scheme. A professional will know every trick in the book, allowing the very last cubic centimetre of the scheme to be utilized. The choice of materials, and therefore the palette of

design opportunities, increases on a yearly basis to the power of ten, so sitting down with someone who can offer an extensive product and finishes library makes obvious sense. It not only saves you shoe leather but also provides you with a design springboard and, simultaneously, serves as an aesthetic regulator for every element of the design.

A few years ago, designers were perceived as beings whose sole purpose in life was to sell stuff to unsuspecting people that they didn't want, at prices they didn't want to pay. How things have changed! We designers are now, thank goodness, recognized as a largely practical bunch, whose principle purpose is to facilitate our clients' ideas, adding spice where necessary, but essentially being on hand for advice, help and the project management of the scheme.

Style versus practicality

For the ultimate kitchen, one has to balance looks and technology, high-impact design and day-to-day practicality. Simple things, such as making sure that you can get a hot pan from the cooker to the sink in one easy motion, or that you can reach to the fridge while standing at the chopping block without dislocating a shoulder are, of course, immensely important.

This simple and straightforward policy comes with a name, 'The Kitchen Triangle'. It's the imaginary geometry that links the three most used pieces of equipment in a kitchen – the cooker, sink and fridge – within a three-step space. Remember, too, that anything specified for use in a kitchen has to be absolutely durable; it is the one space in your house that will suffer all that a family can throw at it.

above top Your kitchen needn't be a boring slave to tradition and functionality, it can be as colourful and exciting as any other room in the house.

above bottom Simplicity needn't be that simple. There's room for style even in a 'minimalist' scheme.

top left
Treating kitchens to colour is a good way of ensuring they feel more like a room and less like a machine. Blue is often perceived as an inappropriate colour next to food, yet surely French navy as a background to citrus lemon is perfect.

middle left Throw in a zingy accent to bring succulence into the scheme.

bottom left
Steels, aluminium, chrome and white metals in general have become the most popular choices as kitchen accents over the past few years.

CHOOSING YOUR SCHEME

Having dwelt on the constraints of kitchen design, it would be very easy to raise one's eyes to heaven and succumb to the simple option, settling for a battleship-grey colour scheme. It may well be as practical as a nuclear submarine, but that rather misses the point. Don't forget just how much time you spend in the kitchen from day to day, and bear in mind that it needs to be a space in which you feel relaxed and completely at home.

Materials

My personal philosophy about kitchen design is to try and integrate the decorative elements, just as you would in any other room. The predominance of operating-theatre stainless steel during the 1990s gave a lot of people a bit of an aesthetic fright, signalling as it did that the kitchen was a machine and that we were but cogs. The advent of the Shaker style softened the approach (thank goodness), but induced in us all a semi-rural dreamstate from which I think, perhaps, it has been hard to move on.

Certainly, natural materials are king in the kitchen as far as contemporary magazines go – which is, in fact, far enough. Most synthetic artefacts and materials do, over time, degrade and look terrible. Anything natural ages much more gracefully, and some natural materials, such as wood and rubber, have an in-built ability to 'self-heal', at least to some extent.

When choosing materials for the kitchen, always select those that you think you're going to enjoy over a

above Blue is a traditional and
dependable kitchen style...

above ...but never limit yourself, particularly if
pink is your thing.

period of time. It's a great temptation to be seduced
by magazines showing fun finishes in trendy fashion
colours, but how long will it last? And, more
importantly: for how long will you personally love
it, once the trend is over?

Personalize your space

As with most rooms, the secret of a good kitchen is not
arcane, it does not rely on any mystical knowledge or
even skip-loads of design talent. But it does hinge on
you, the occupier, making up your mind. Depending on
your requirements, what you want to say about yourself
with your kitchen should be as personal a statement as
your living room or bedroom, whether it says uptown
urbanite or rural recluse.

If nothing else, I hope that *Home Front* has
demonstrated that there is no right way, no wrong way,
but only your way. And whatever it is that you see your
kitchen being, then please find the courage to do it.
Be expressive, be yourself and enjoy your kitchen.

inside

KITCHEN LIVING

above Restful blues enlivened by off-whites are balanced by a rich dark floor and the rather glamorously sparkling work surface.

CREATING A CHILD-FRIENDLY SPACE

Preparing food in a poorly-planned kitchen, with one ear constantly pricked for the inevitable crash, bang and squeal of a child up to no good, strikes a chord with so many of us. In such circumstances, cooking is a chore, so it's important to create a space that allows you to prepare food unperturbed by what's happening elsewhere.

Kate's mother had a farmhouse in France, and it was during her regular stays there that she felt she could truly unwind; she had enough space there to conjure up glorious food, while her son, Isaac, played at her feet. I decided on a solution that works well in many homes; to open up the kitchen into another room, creating a space that would double as a dining room and a place for a child to play within view.

Here, as in most Edwardian houses, the kitchen was small, meanly proportioned and outside the main circulation space of the ground floor. The first thing to do was to remove as much as possible of the wall that divided the kitchen and dining room. Taking walls out is a messy and complicated business; it requires a structural engineer to inspect the building and specify the necessary load-bearing supports. It also needs an inspection by the local Building Control Office to ensure the work is safe.

In some cases, rather than removing a wall entirely, it's easier and more effective to create a large aperture centred on both rooms, to create formal views from one end to another. This is what I did here, and we also benefitted from not losing a lot of storage space by removing all of a wall on which we could hang cupboards.

The Brief

Kate needed more space and a new, convenient kitchen layout to escape the claustrophobic feeling of enclosure; in all, her kitchen was an area that was more burden than retreat. As a busy PR with a lively 2-year-old son, Isaac, Kate wanted time for herself away from the responsibilities of work and motherhood, a place where she could rekindle her love of cooking, while Isaac had room to pursue his own activities. A large section of the dividing wall was removed to incorporate the rarely used dining room into the kitchen.

Their Requirements

The room had to be durable and practical, but also had to function as a retreat from a hectic lifestyle and have a tangibly romantic mood, redolent of Kate's stays in her mother's farmhouse in France. From the outset, Kate wanted a suitably easy-going backdrop to the inevitable clutter of a busy working mother and an active toddler.

The Materials

Dark chocolate-brown floorboards, pale blue painted walls and timber panelling would all reflect the rural charm of a French farmhouse.

RURAL STYLE

Giving the kitchen a rural veneer is a popular choice for busy families. The easy-going, organic atmosphere of kitchens that develop their style through years of practical use, makes for highly seductive schemes in which one simply gets on with life, as opposed to chasing one's tail in a constant attempt to live up to a more contrived look.

Based predominantly on natural materials, the rural kitchen is updated by the delicate handling of synthetic materials. Reflective stainless steel modernizes the look, as well as reflecting, and therefore maximizing, available light. As so often in interior design, success comes from balance. Modern shapes in traditional or rustic materials wear their influences lightly, as do traditional forms in modern finishes. The true joy of this kind of decorating is the *laissez faire* attitude one can adopt to clutter. Willow baskets stuffed with receipts, action man parts and string don't act as a nagging spectre at the feast in the way they do in more controlled, modern schemes.

The colour scheme was to be soft French blues (perfect against the rich, dark floor), with a kitchen planned for convenience and a look that mingled traditional and contemporary elements.

below left Granite work surfaces are tough and practical. The routed surface obviates the need for a drainer by the sink.

below right Enamel handles are a soft visual option in a truly French way.

top Simple modern furniture shapes with an interesting texture bring the scheme to life.

bottom The scheme was styled with objects that were witty as well as stylish.

The rural kitchen

To create an organic feel that accommodates the lack of symmetry inherent in any kitchen layout, you can superimpose over the carefully-designed layout a scheme for cupboard doors. This gives a mismatched look, with the panel detail varying from cupboard to cupboard. We also used handmade tiles in blue and ivory for the kitchen, to give it a rustic, traditional feel, and installed a new stained-glass window above the sink to bring colour and an old-fashioned ambience to the room.

The flooring

Rich, dark finishes can act as reassuring counterpoints to paler colours, reinforcing the delicacy and pale tonality of lighter shades. In this room we used a bitter chocolate-coloured floor, which was an aesthetic joy when set in its soft blue context. The benefits of using this dark colour adjacent to French windows opening out into the garden, as we did here, are obvious, but the intensity of reflected light from a dark but reflective finish may surprise you.

The walls

In the old dining room – soon to be reincarnated as a *chambre de petit dejeuner* (breakfast room!) – I specified simple panelling using softwood uprights and a timber cornice for a simple, modernized Arts and Crafts look. Above each panel, the plaster was cut and then chipped off in a square of the same dimensions, exposing the brickwork behind. Painted the same soft ivory as the ceiling, it made a romantic reference to rural architecture and the Gallic love of painted, exposed brickwork.

right Modern craft pieces like these vases bring schemes with a rural nod bang up to date. If you look to add a contemporary twist, focus on the handmade rather than the mass produced.

far right The finished scheme: soft, romantic, rural and bizarrely uncontrived.

One concern that many people have when they consider panelling is that it may be too formal an option, but panels can be used to great effect to create a soft rhythm in a room and a sense of continuity. In this room, they were softened by pale colours and provided the perfect background to the accumulated clutter of family living.

Using fabric in your scheme

Kitchens are often fabric-free zones, which is a shame. A drape of fabric is so useful in softening the angular lines that are prevalent in the kitchen. It can make a space feel more mellow, more lived-in and most importantly, less kitchen-like and utilitarian. Even the lightest, brightest, modern kitchen can look chilly during the day and, worse still, rather institutional once the sun has set over the aluminium work surfaces. Always factor the look of the kitchen at night into your decision-making.

While the messy work continued, I designed and had printed a French *Toile de Jouy*-inspired fabric by specialists, Marino Mills. *Toile de Jouy* was very popular in the eighteenth and nineteenth centuries and is a keynote of French decoration. Normally, rural scenes featuring shepherdesses and broken fences are scattered over the large-scale repeat of the fabric. For Kate, I drew elements important to her and Isaac: chocolate, coffee, playing in the garden and granny's rural idyll in Carcassonne. It was printed in pale, smoky blues and soft coffees on a linen ground, to coordinate with the blue/brown colour scheme.

The finishing touches

A goodly sprinkle of introduced clutter never goes amiss in this kind of context; interesting textures, objects that introduce an accent colour, even specifically themed pieces give the scheme a kick start. It's like creating a framework around which the clutter of daily life can grow like beans on a cane.

Curtains sorted, decorating done, all that remained were the finishing touches – a coat of wax polish on the emulsion that was used to decorate the panelling, a new stained-glass window above the sink and a framed print by Icelandic artist, Carolina Larasdotir, to have pride of place in the breakfast room.

A LOOK AT THE DETAILS

A deep, stainless steel extractor hood has been used here to make an architectural statement in its own right, as well as performing a very practical function.

Linen colours and textures are the perfect fabric solutions in this kind of scheme. They create a seductive, homespun softness that is both practical and aesthetic.

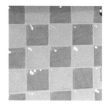
Blue and white handmade tiles used as a chequerboard splashback added a rural feel to the kitchen and called to mind French bistros and the Gallic love of food.

A deep plate shelf is a traditional rural touch that provides extra storage as well as an additional display surface. The square panels, which expose painted brick above the panelling, create an added dimension and an interplay of light and shade.

The kitchen unit doors have random panels to offset the lack of symmetry that is inherent in most kitchens, and to provide the organic feeling of rural design. Ceramic handles complete the effect.

Panelling in this context works on two levels; as a practical, durable wall surface and as an architectural mechanism that introduces an underlying sense of rhythm to the scheme.

inside THE SOCIABLE KITCHEN

above The scheme was an easy-going, friendly mixture of Mexican colours, textures and more contemporary European finishes.

opposite Hot and sassy, all that pink was begging for silver as a cool down.

UNIFYING YOUR SPACE

Deciding to remove a wall that separates two spaces is easy, but creating a unified look for the space that results takes more thought. If, as here, you want your new, open area to be the heart of the house, and want the kitchen not to feel too 'kitcheny', but to be considered as a room in its own right, its design should reflect and coordinate with the scheme designed for the dining room.

We achieved this here through use of colour and flooring. A jump from one floor finish to another creates an obvious visual threshold, over which one has – literally and psychologically – to step. Taking the same materials through the space, either on the floor or the walls, regardless of boundaries, is the most straightforward way of stating 'this is one big room rather than two knocked together'.

The dining and kitchen areas were unified by a new, pale stone floor that was the perfect surface to take underfloor heating, creating a uniformly warm and cosy experience for bare feet.

Unifying through colour

Strong colours leap forward whilst paler colours tend to recede. One is faced, therefore, with a choice when deciding on a colour scheme for a space – do I want my walls to come towards me, or to back away from me?

In large areas, one can afford to play a clever game; using rich, saturated hues in specific areas for in-your-face excitement, while harmonizing the majority of the

The Brief

Nick and Imy were looking for a fusion style that reflected Imy's Mexican heritage and Nick's British upbringing and which struck a perfect balance between the reserved practicality of the British and the salsa-hot exoticism of central America. The existing kitchen, although on the small and dark side, had been relatively well planned, but the dining room next door felt unloved and uninhabited. They wanted to be able to use both in the most efficient way possible. Colour and mood were as important as practicality.

Their Requirements

The mood should be soft and warm but, at the same time, refined and flexible. They wanted a style that could be classed as 'salsa-modern', mingling wit, elegance and energy with the contemporary. They envisaged using the space for large parties, so a flexible arrangement of furniture was fundamental.

The Materials

Imy originally said she'd like acres of stainless steel in her kitchen, which rather worried me on a practical level. I knew that accenting the scheme with steel would help to balance the hot colours and the rough textures of stone, brick and timber so, wherever I could, I slipped in a stainless steel detail. The slick finish of the laminate patchwork doors was a real innovation, adding spicy colour accents to a traditional layout that was executed in highly modern materials.

space with paler colours to create a feeling of distance. From the outset, both Nick and Imy claimed a love of strong colour and, for Imy in particular, pink spelled Mexico. The colour pink can be cloying and, perversely, can create a rather cold effect, especially when there are blue notes in the mix, so it is worth playing around with pink pigments until you have created a shade that you can see will work.

Hot colours need confident handling, so think about painting the majority of a wall area in a pale colour, such as white, to create a neutral framework for the imposition of hot corals and sugar pinks. In this design we used an almost coral 'Imy Pink', which was specially mixed for her. We used it for large colour blocks throughout both areas to create impact against the ubiquitous, chalk-white background that I had specified to lighten the scheme.

The rich, warm shade of the main body of pink in the room was sufficiently well balanced with a lot of orange and not much violet – using pink against pink in such an energetic, eccentric way can create an invigorating accent for the scheme.

right The scheme abounded in detail and colour, which Imy, with her artist's eye, could take continuing pleasure from. The wood-burning stove in a circular painted brick aperture with a tiled hearth brought a specifically Mexican reference into the mix.

Unifying through materials

The secret to unifying a large space is to think of the area as a salad – it must be balanced and mixed well. Introducing an element in one area presupposes that the element will be mirrored elsewhere in the scheme. The look of Nick and Imy's kitchen/dining room relied on many elements – used in moderation throughout – for an easy-going, elegantly cluttered effect. With a more simplistic design approach, it is easier to take two or three finishes and a couple of colours and calculate a cubic percentage that will define what goes where and how much you need.

In this design, we installed a stone work surface to coordinate with the floor, and the 'patchwork' motif on the door fronts was made up of narrow strips of laminate in contrasting pinks. The professional range-style cooker was fitted as the centrepiece for the kitchen, positioned within the original chimney breast.

The stainless steel against the softer texture of the painted brick created a surprising effect, balancing contrasting visual textures. The stainless steel theme was continued in the stubby legs of the kitchen units (putting base units on legs is a good tip; it makes the available space in a kitchen feel greater), and on the pivoting island unit, which I had designed to swing between the kitchen and dining area.

Always the elements were contrasted and balanced, hard stone against soft brickwork, sleek chalk-coloured laminate against harsh pinks, steel against canvas. By mingling textures in this way, the scheme felt organic, easy-going and lovable.

Incorporating ethnic style

The days of in-your-face rooms, which, after all, lack a certain subtlety, are drawing to a close. A few years ago, the nation abounded with Mexican-style kitchens that wore their obvious references rather too proudly. In a scheme like this one, success comes from understanding the elements of Mexican style and then reinterpreting them, refining them, even abstracting them, until they feel new and fresh.

The history of design is littered with exotic influences from China to Japan, Scandinavia to Mexico, and as these styles become better and better understood, they become seamlessly absorbed into British design. Nick and Imy wanted, and indeed got, a sprinkling of overtly Mexican references, but the atmosphere of the room remains contemporary.

Mexican-inspired motifs cropped up everywhere. We used hand-painted tiles in pink and chalk, instead of skirting boards. Tiling is rarely seen outside bathrooms and kitchens in the UK, and almost never in dining rooms, but tiled skirtings and architraves are traditional in Mediterranean countries and their use travelled to Mexico with the Spanish.

We also incorporated hand-wrought tine mirrors as light fittings, and the large, ornate, silver-leafed candlesticks alluded to the heavy Baroque style that was favoured by Spanish Mexicans in the nineteenth century. The more ornate elements and specially commissioned, hand-crafted pieces were carefully balanced by the clean, contemporary lines that were used throughout.

above Stronger, more daring pinks, work well in this context as small-scale accent notes.

right The boundary between dining area and kitchen is successfully blurred, allowing a space of this size to accommodate colour and detail. The stepped storage unit beneath the intruding stairwell was a successful solution to a cramped, oddly shaped space.

A space for entertaining

The swivelling breakfast bar, with its stone work surface and integrated storage, creates a highly social focus for the area, providing dinner party guests who arrive early with somewhere to sit and shell peas without getting under their hosts' feet. It also acts as a decompression chamber between the guests' space – the dining area – and the engine room of the dinner party – the kitchen.

The dining room would regularly form the backdrop to large dinner parties, so the dining table, a monster of a thing, was designed to seat twelve people in comfort. The top of the table was constructed from blocks of end-grain softwood that were stained a rich, dark brown and set into paler framework for contrast.

The final scheme balanced the personalities of two different people, along with the flavour of two separate cultures, while remaining light and contemporary.

There was plenty of detail and interest, but the effect stopped short of clutter, achieving an easy-going yet glamorous family atmosphere instead.

Lighting

Sprinkling the ceiling with low-voltage halogen lights is an excellent way of boosting light levels. Halogen provides a bright, clean light that has a spectrum similar to that of natural daylight, which is useful in balancing the rather warmer, more amber glow of tungsten. I always feel it's important to offer a choice of both, because areas like this have to accommodate many levels of activity by a variety of personalities.

In this situation, constantly high light levels would be both undesirable and uncomfortable, so several low-voltage, halogen-lit scenarios were installed to provide a choice of bright working light, subdued eating light or romantic, low-level snogging light.

A LOOK AT THE DETAILS

 Specially commissioned, mirrored light fittings had sparkle on their side. The form was based on traditional Hispanic sunburst motifs, so they echo the ornate Hispanic-Baroque candle stands perfectly.

 Painted brickwork is a soft, organic wall finish that acts here as a counterpoint to the slick use of reflective stainless steel. Exposed brickwork was a 1970s kitchen favourite, but painting it this pale, subtle colour brings it right up to date.

 A patchwork of laminates in infinite pinks establishes an energetic but moderated colour palette. Kitchen-unit fronts can be rather flat, bland affairs, but here they work as part of an overall scheme.

 The judicious use of honey-coloured timber (here defining the stepped effect of the storage unit) brings a note of warmth to the scheme, which helps to balance the light, bright colour palette.

 Richer colours spring forward to meet the eye, so bordering colour blocks in paler, receding colours plays a game of *trompe l'oeil*, bringing the panel forward visually, while pushing the wall back.

 Real 'screaming pink' accents are great for enlivening a scheme. But remember to limit their scale, as we have here, to attain balance between the visual impact of such eye-catching hues with the space they take up.

inside RETRO DINING

A CIRCULAR KITCHEN

On the surface, it sounds like one of the most perversely 'designerish' things to do: slap a circular kitchen into a square space – round pegs and square holes spring to mind – but, in this instance, there were some very persuasive practical benefits to this kitchen layout.

Imagine the flight deck of an aeroplane – everything within fingertip reach of the pilot – then compare with a square kitchen in which the fridge is at the other end of a diagonal path from the cooker, and the sink is on the other side of the room from the dishwasher. In these terms, rounding off the corners suddenly makes sense – there are now no right angles to attract and capture dirt, and no difficult corners into which appliances and storage have to be squeezed.

Having said all of that, however, it is not merely a practical solution: the aesthetic impact of a curvy, circular kitchen cannot be underestimated. The project, in fact, covered two areas: the kitchen and the adjacent breakfast room, which had a glazed, conservatory-style ceiling. The breakfast room had loads of character and plenty of architecture, so I could adopt a relatively softly-softly approach to the design, while, of course, making sure that it didn't feel like a poor relation next to the gorgeousness that I planned for the kitchen.

The breakfast room conservatory

A glass roof is a wonderful addition to any room, allowing the light to simply pour in. It is a particularly clever idea for a breakfast room, in as much as you can sit and read the paper in the morning and almost

above The streamlined and curvy kitchen, part-Sputnik, part-Wonderbra.

opposite The light, bright breakfast room required an aesthetic change of gear.

The Brief

To create a convenient, good-looking kitchen and breakfast room space that would suit a growing family with a modern outlook. Available space had to be maximized and, bearing in mind how tall Julie is, the work surfaces had to be at a level that was comfortable for her to use. The dark kitchen needed to be very well lit, while the bright conservatory breakfast room had to be shielded from the sun.

The Requirements

A modern, yet not clinically contemporary look was required. Colour, in a subdued yet invigorating palette, was to be used to bring life and excitement, while decorative elements, including any patternwork, had to have a geometric quality. For practical reasons, a dark floor was a must for a room so close to the garden. The restrained use of 1950s detailing was to be included for a touch of retro glamour.

The Materials

Since colour was to play a major role, the kitchen units were to be painted. Pyrolave, a sexy French worksurface material, made from enamelled lava, would create a bold accent to be offset against a dark-stained kitchen floor. Bold splashes of colour would be introduced by means of custom-designed contemporary glass panels.

believe that you are in much sunnier climes. I had to address one real drawback, though: one that is shared by all glass-roofed spaces – how to shield the occupants from the sun when, on the rare occasions it decided to shine, heat and light streamed through the roof.

Blinds are by far the easiest solution, and here I used canvas ones that owed much to the sail maker's art. They proved ideal, since they also improved the acoustics in this rather echoing room and made the space feel much softer and cosier on rainy days.

I felt that I needed to inject a little contemporary pattern to prevent the scheme from feeling too hard-edged and modern. To achieve this, I decided to design a bespoke fabric for the blinds, and to incorporate a series of unmatched motifs that would be printed on the backs of the brightly coloured bentwood chairs. For inspiration, I researched the work of Lucienne Day, one of Britain's foremost textile designers, whose work shaped so much post-war design and whose textiles most famously brought life, pattern and colour to the 1951 Festival of Britain.

right Chartreuse
accented by blue with
glass artpieces.

far right The fabulous
Pyrolave worksurface was
cast with runnels to act
as a drainer.

The dining space

The problem with most dining spaces is that, for much
of the time, we need to seat just a few people, but at
other times, we want to entertain and invite more
people round than we really have room for. A large table
is often the obvious answer, but this can be irritating if
it takes up the whole room when the space is needed
for other activities.

There are tables on the market that extend by means
of leaf inserts, or by flaps that lift up at either end but,
in this case, I came up with a cunning plan. I designed a
table that was made up of three separate sections. This
meant that it could be arranged in several permutations,
from long and thin for extended family parties, to short
and fat for dining alone. It could also serve as a single
table in the middle of the room, while the other two
sections acted as console tables against the walls.

DESIGNING THE KITCHEN

Creating a kitchen is a specialist discipline, and making
a circular kitchen required a really good kitchen
designer who could think laterally. In situations like
this, it's a good idea to call in the experts, and so I
brought in Lynne, of Febo Design, who came over the
horizon like the seventh cavalry. I had provided her with
a set of drawings to show the look I required, but I felt
rather guilty at dumping the whole lot on her desk
without attempting to resolve the geometry, or how the
water would reach the sink, or the gas the hob.

Expert that she is, she rose to the challenge and
quickly integrated all that I wanted the kitchen to

be with the tricky issues of use and practicality.
Designing a kitchen has so many considerations to be
taken into account – plumbing, gas, electricity and
other practical, day-to-day issues – that it is never a bad
idea to call in the experts. Although, as a designer,
I felt a little uncomfortable at passing the job over to
another designer, I knew that the work would be done
smoothly and expertly. But anyway, guilt is a wasted
emotion, so don't feel bad about getting in the
professionals. It removes the headache of the project
and leaves you with time to think about the details of
the room, rather than the more mundane aspects, such
as storage and layout.

The finished kitchen worked really well. The sliding
doors (see page 42) were fantastic, both aesthetically,
because they followed the curve of the base units, and
practically, as they slid from one side to the other,
allowing access deep within the cupboards without
leaning or straining.

The 'kitchen triangle' rule (see page 23) was put to
great effect here, and the proximity of the sink to the
oven, fridge and hotplate minimized the distance to
carry a big, hot pan of boiling water. It's an important
part of kitchen design and a rule that is definitely worth
keeping if you spend a lot of time cooking.

Kitchen materials

There is a huge variety of materials available for work
surfaces, from granite to wood to laminates, which all
have their pros and cons. Each is suitable for specific
uses, so sit down with a kitchen designer and find one

right The brightly-coloured glass splashback became an art piece in its own right.

that suits you, your design and budget best. For this kitchen, I had fallen in love with a rather revolutionary work-surface material called Pyrolave, which is manufactured in France. It is made from volcanic rock that is cut to shape and then enamelled in rich, vibrant colours. Of course, my work surface needed to be circular and, since it was arriving after the curved walls and the units were installed, it would have to fit into place like a glove, first time. Because of the nature of the material, there would be absolutely no room to manoeuvre, and no chance of cutting it down if it was too long, or padding it out if it was too short.

Introducing colour

I had chosen a vibrant French navy for the Pyrolave, to act as a sassy accent against one of my favourite kitchen colours, cucumber green. Slightly yellow greens, such as cucumber or Chartreuse (after the booze) are restful and calming, but they are still warm, even on overcast, grey days.

So the curved units and walls were coloured in a series of cucumber shades, and the scheme very much started to take shape. To get square, rigid tiles to meet the required radius of my curves would have been almost impossible. What was needed was a rigid material that could be cast exactly into the curve and Pyrolave fitted the bill perfectly.

left Simple, restrained objects with a mid-20th century twist.

To go behind the hob, I designed a glass splashback in bright, upbeat colours – lime-green, orange and yellow – on a rich blue ground. In the breakfast room, I used this device as an accent and to provide a sense of continuity. I designed three large panels of coloured glass with abstract blocks of greens, whites, oranges and blues, to be mounted as art pieces on the walls. These were displayed an inch or so away from the walls on chromed spaces, so that, as the light hit them, coloured reflections would be cast through the glass onto the wall behind.

A LOOK AT THE DETAILS

Traditionally, eye-line ovens are part of an integrated unit, sometimes 'stacked' above another appliance, such as a grill. It's unusual to have one above a section of work surface but, in fact, it's very practical. Dishes can be transferred from the oven to the work surface in one easy movement and the circular work surface could remain continuous.

The modern light fitting screams 'Sputnik', with its space-age, illuminated globes on chromed arms. I felt this fitting added a lot to the circular space – drawing attention to the curve without cluttering the ceiling with unnecessary detail. The whole piece appears to orbit the centre of the room, another reference to the 1950s space-race.

Integrally lit display niches not only provide extra storage at high level, they also punctuate the curved wall, giving a less dense effect. Simple, box-like niches set into stud walls are a real keynote of modernist design, but ultimately derive from ancient sources in Egypt and Greece.

Sliding doors were a real keynote of 1950s kitchen design, but have been neglected ever since. It's a shame, because they're so convenient if space is at a premium, when the last thing you need are hinged doors opening into your valuable working area. Here, sliding doors are a dream; they allow access to the very back of the cupboards.

This glass splashback, specially commissioned from Febo Design, is a chic alternative to tiling. The glass was constructed to follow the line of the curve, and the accent colours used elsewhere in the kitchen – cobalt blue, cadmium orange and lime green – add pattern detail and interest in bold, concentric spots.

The central island unit created an additional work surface with an integrated chopping board. As a piece of furniture, it could become a visual and practical encumbrance if fixed; so we put it on heavy duty castors, allowing it to be moved around the kitchen, to create a valuable surface wherever it is needed most.

insideout
BEDROOMS

THE BEDROOM THEN AND NOW

Historically speaking, the bedroom has undergone a major revolution in the 20th century. The 18th century nobleman would have had access to three bedrooms, which he would use throughout the course of the night.

The first, a grand ceremonial space with an ornate state bed, would be called into play as an official backdrop for saying goodnight to his retinue – a courtly and choreographed ballet of manners. After the curtains on his four-poster had been drawn, and the last of his hangers-on had left, he himself would leave to make full use of the next bedroom belonging either to his wife (if an heir was required) or his mistress.

There were, of course, plenty of louche aristos who had the energy to visit both ladies (at least!) before retiring to the last bedroom of the night. This was a far smaller, more intimate chamber bedecked with favourite possessions, where the rake would flop, exhausted, into a simpler, more comfortable bed. In the morning, his valet would wash and shave him and then lead him back to the state bedchamber to be officially 'woken' during the ceremony of the 'levée' or 'rising', when his chattering retinue would be back petitioning for favours or looking for gossip.

It was as unusual then for husband and wife to sleep in the same bed as it is now for them to occupy separate bedrooms in separate wings. Increased informality and intimacy, combined with a reduced scale of living, has created the modern bedroom.

As with dining rooms, bedrooms are most often enjoyed at night, so lighting becomes a major creative element.

For us, interior design is a new deregulated, democratized passion that begs to be treated in a personal, individual way.

Private spaces

For us grown-ups there can be no doubt that bedrooms are romantic spaces. Forgive me for stating the obvious, but my point is that, in decorative terms, the way a bedroom is designed often tells a story and, nine times out of ten, is really quite revealing about its occupants. Obviously it's not a public area, so personal statements are more likely in the bedroom than in any other area, except perhaps the bathroom. Bedroom furniture can be kept to a basic minimum: bed, dressing-table and wardrobe. Alternatively, the bedroom can take all that you throw at it in furniture terms and probably more.

Design considerations

Darker, richer colours might typify a bedroom scheme in a household where pale, pebble shades or whites predominate elsewhere. Unlike any other space in the house, bedrooms receive light wear. Decorating kitchens and bathrooms requires a practical, durable mindset. Living rooms and halls are likely to receive high volumes of traffic, whereas the bedroom is really down to you and your partner.

Rest, peace and tranquillity are the most obvious preoccupations, but there are more people than you'd realize who like the reverse: energetic, sumptuous, stimulating, decorative schemes that wake you up in the morning and probably keep you up all night.

opposite Always make room for glamour.

above Bedrooms are the ultimate escape and, for many, a bit of Hollywood never goes amiss after a working day spent in front of a VDU.

left Sophistication and control typify many of today's bedroom schemes.

left Always consider texture when choosing your bedlinen.

below A really rather restrained outing for us, but successful in its own right.

One feature of bedroom decoration a lot of us have to consider is storage. A few generations back, when people mostly occupied larger areas, dressing rooms could be used to store clothes. These days, winter and summer wardrobes, golf clubs, suitcases, shoes, jocks and socks all need to be squeezed into the rooms in which we sleep.

THE SPARE BEDROOM

Spare bedrooms are an interesting topic in their own right. Most of us can come home safe in the knowledge that we know we have a bed for the night and a designated room in which to sleep. The spare bedroom, however, often has a far more confused identity.

Setting aside a room that will be used only now and then is becoming increasingly difficult to justify, when every square inch of every square foot we occupy needs to pay its way. The spare room so often becomes the one area in the house that silts up like a seldom-used estuary as space runs out in wardrobes, attics or boot cupboards. The guest bed quickly becomes a

above Space 1999 meets lack of space 2001.

top right Bunk beds for astronauty astronauts.

dumping ground, and the dressing table a makeshift computer desk. I can't help feeling there's a lot to be said for factoring multi-tasking into the layout and design of the spare room.

Forget about all the finishing touches until you have squeezed every last drop of storage space out of the room. Think about cunning ways of integrating the additional activities that have found a home in the spare room that won't mean compromising the aesthetics. Computers can be hidden behind screens; craft or hobby activities kept in willow baskets or painted storage boxes; exercise equipment can be stored beneath beds or inside wardrobe space. Then, and only then, start thinking about how you're going to make the room a restful background to the mother-in-law's snoring!

The bedroom offers scope to make that personal statement in a more emphatic way than anywhere else in the house. If you want it minimal – go for zeroism; if you want it opulent – go for ultra-baroque with knobs on. If you want it romantic – well, only you know your upper limit and – if you want my advice – when you've found it, exceed it in style.

above Citrus funky homework helpers.

inside

ROOM WITH A VIEW

above When in its daytime mood, the room felt tailored and masculine, while at night, satin and fine wool added highlights of feminine glamour.

opposite left The new pergola and restored windows.

opposite right A bit of dignified plant propping on the roof garden.

DESIGNING IN A PERIOD PROPERTY

Many people only dream of owning a really individual period property but, for those of us who achieve the dream, any home improvements do need to be considered carefully and carried out sympathetically. In this case, we were asked to design a rooftop bedroom and solarium space in an architecturally important building, Blue Rails. The house is mentioned in many of the books on 20th-Century architecture and, as such, demanded sensitive handling. An extraordinary pre-war statement of modern optimism in a new technological age, Blue Rails typified all the features of Art Deco. Or did it?

Approaching interior design in any building with a bit of character or history to it can be daunting. One has to make a basic, pretty fundamental decision, which is whether you or the house are going to win; which personality is going to be expressed in the way the rooms look? Many people buy period homes because they love the idea of integrating themselves into the traditions of the previous inhabitants. Some have more bravura, looking to impose their tastes, their preoccupations, and their individuality onto the existing architecture.

Personally, I feel either approach is legitimate, although for those of a forceful decorating disposition, it is essential they consider long and hard before thoughtlessly removing architectural elements. So, if a fireplace or light fitting does not accord with the design identity one wishes to express within the space, by all means take them away, but make sure they are undamaged and stored somewhere on site for a future generation whose taste they might suit.

There are legal constraints on what you can and can't do in some old buildings, and there are several grades of listed buildings with various levels of constraint. The local planning authority will always advise you. The up-side is that, in some cases, grants are available to help with restoration work, about which, again, the local authority will be able to provide information.

Restoration

If you do decide to reflect the style of your period home in your interior design, the restoration of original features may play an important part in your plans. At Blue Rails, our first job was a touch of restoration. The original Crittel windows' narrow glazing bars in metal were in relatively good condition, but required a bit of sorting out here and there. Crittel windows were

The Brief

Heather and Simon wanted to reincarnate an unloved and under-used rooftop room with little character into a glamorous master bedroom that could become an elegant, elevated garden room by day. A rooftop pergola, obvious in original photographs of the house, was to be reinstated (but redesigned) to offer shady areas in the roof-terrace garden. A major part of the brief was to respect the age and character of the house, exploring and possibly evolving the 1930s style to give it a modern twist.

Their Requirements

It needed to be luxurious and intelligent and incorporate some space-saving solutions. It should be a perfect environment for sun worshippers that wouldn't get too hot or too cold. During the day, with sun streaming through the windows and impressive views of Luton, it should present a holiday hideaway feel. At night, it should be cosy, comfortable and indulgent.

The Materials

Many of the materials had to refer directly to the period of the house, so chrome sprang to mind instantly. The Moderne period was well-known for celebrating the machine and man-made plastics, but it also took delight in the sleekest of natural materials.

left With the bed down, two bedside niches were renovated to house lamps, alarm clocks, books and night-time clutter.

an architectural innovation at the time, allowing more light into a room than conventional timber frames.

The 1930s was a decade obsessed with sunlight, hence the vogue for solariums. Solariums were largely glazed rooms, often built onto flat roofs, designed for enjoyment of the healing benefits of the sun's rays, which, according to health gurus of the time, were ideal for nurseries or sick rooms.

For this project, I designed two major architectural elements that reflected the original features. The first, a new pergola, which replaced the original wooden one on the terrace that extended out from this rooftop room,

gave me immense pleasure as it began to take shape. There is something lovely about restoring to a building an important element that is visible from the street and which has been lost from the house for decades. In this case, slightly cheekily, I increased the proportions of the pergola from the original elevations, but it was a sneaky compromise that paid off. It was constructed in white-painted timber with discreetly integrated lighting.

On the roof terrace, where load-bearing was a critical consideration, I designed a series of semicircular planters made in lightweight fibreglass that rose up in curvaceous tiers. One of the most exciting new materials

far left The graphically designed rug in chic black on white and the sleekly inlaid panelling continue the ocean liner feel.

left Comfort and convenience are necessities; we installed a switch system that meant the lights could be turned off from the bed without having to get up once ready for slumber.

right I designed a chrome, floor-standing lamp with a series of opaque glass tubular shades arranged in an inverted triangle. It had overtones of Art Deco cinemas with its sparse, machine-age detailing, and looked very at home.

of the 1920s and 30s was cast concrete, so the planters were painted with a sand-textured, exterior masonry paint as a textural back-reference to the Moderne age's love of concrete.

Storage with style

In a room that will have a life beyond being simply a bedroom and where space is at a premium, you may want to consider clever ways of using the space most effectively. It was important here to be able to put away the bed in the room, so that Heather and Simon could make the most of the space when they weren't sleeping. I decided on a solution that was practical as well as in keeping with the period.

Concealed flap-down beds were a space-saving innovation of the 1930s and called to mind pre-war ocean-going liners or exotic, first-class railway Pullmans. But the bed threw up more than a few design problems. For a start, when folded away, it would be a rather ugly, solid lump of timber. So this, I decided, should be integrated as a major element by panelling the entire wall in pale timber with inlaid bands of darker wood veneers.

Period details

Even if you decide not to go the whole hog and restore your home to its original condition, you can incorporate period details into your scheme to give an accent of the age. I found records of some of the original decorative elements, such as fabrics and furniture, which I used to inspire my scheme. From the documents, I discovered that there had been fabrics with a repeated circular motif, so I decided to intersperse these with the stripes on the panelling, as well as using them as a design inspiration for sun curtains. Panels of lightweight, opaque white fabric were woven with translucent bands and circles, allowing soft shafts of light to shimmer through on sunny days. At night, blackout roller blinds could be called into play, which are wonderful if you don't want to be woken at dawn, and even better if your lifestyle demands that you must sleep during the day.

When lowered, the hard timber exterior of the bed revealed a soft woollen heart. Sky-blue wool blanketing was used to upholster the bed's backboard in comfortable, deeply buttoned squares. The flash of blue carried through to the Hollywood-glamorous, hand-quilted silk eiderdown for maximum luxury and comfort. For the middle of the room, I commissioned a circular rug with a black and white motif.

Lighting was provided by a free-standing chrome lamp with illuminated tubes that followed a lazy 'S' floor plan. The effect was decidedly 1930s and, to make the room as convenient as possible, a switching system was installed so that all lights, both inside and outside, could be switched on and off from the bed.

A LOOK AT THE DETAILS

Light timber panelling was used across the bed wall to accommodate the flap-down bed when not in use. For a bit of 1930s glamour, darker wood veneers were used as a streamlined inlay of circles and lines.

On the roof garden, weight was a prime consideration. Decking created a walkway beneath the pergola, and lightweight fibreglass planters, in a streamlined, Moderne shape, were painted with granular masonry paint to look like cast concrete.

Like those of an ocean-going liner or first-class Pullman, glass vases in metal brackets were mounted on either side of the bed to avoid cluttering up surfaces with extraneous objects.

Beneath the pergola, a 21st century version of Lloyd Loom furniture (a favourite in the 1930s) offered comfortable, lightweight seating that would also grace the solarium during the day.

A replacement pergola was installed, inspired by original photographs, but rescaled to fit the proportions of the white-painted, timber barge boards running around the perimeter of the solarium roof.

When the bed was open, soft, blue woollen blanketing was revealed. Boldly-quilted as a comfortable headboard, it was ideal for night-time reading, or simply looking out through the window to enjoy the view.

inside  WORK AND REST

above A cosy glow ready for bed, with a convenient lavatory/shower room concealed beyond the jib door.

opposite The same room during office hours, crisp, neat and ready for business.

PROBLEM SPACES

Attic rooms can be cosy and romantic, but they do set up all sorts of problems from practical and design points of view. One of the most obvious problems encountered in attics is, of course, headroom. Attic spaces are limited by the pitch of the roof, which often means that one can stand in the middle, but end up crouching at the edges. Attics can also be veritable forests of posts and beams that may have accumulated over the years to support the roof itself.

As a designer, my first consideration in the treatment of an attic space (obviously after practical considerations have been successfully addressed) is the softening of what is essentially a sharply triangular room. The addition of further beams in softer, Gothic shapes has always been a Llewelyn-Bowen favourite for taking the sharpness off an angular space.

Increasing the roof height

Inspecting Sarah's and Malcolm's space, with bizarre little doors everywhere, I felt like Alice in Wonderland. Stripping-out revealed everything and I saw a solution to our head-height problem.

In this situation, always make sure that you consult an expert; there are important structural considerations to be borne in mind when removing rafters, or changing the position of load-bearing supports. Once my ideas were approved and judged viable, the low crossbeams were removed and the weight of the roof was borne by chunky uprights. A new crosspiece, above head height, braced the vertical beams, while purely decorative

curved beams created an elegant, almost Gothic arch and softened the appearance of the structure.

A bathroom, comprising a carefully plumbed-in shower, basin and loo layout, was hidden behind a new stud wall with an acoustic wadding (for obvious reasons) between the layers of plasterboard. Accessed by a concealed 'jib' door, with the dado panelling continued across its surface, this kept the bathroom discreetly concealed during office hours.

Putting new walls into a space needs as much thought as taking old walls out. It's always a good idea to check building regulations when replacing or adding walls because, depending on where they sit within the house, they may be required to meet certified standards of fire retardancy.

Creating the illusion of space

If making structural changes to your roof space is not viable, there are many other ways in which you can make as small a space as this feel less cramped. Because the space was long and narrow, I pinched a trick from

left With so much traditional character in the architecture of the room, the working furniture was sleek, modern and pale in colour with emphatically curved shapes.

far left A typical 19th Century bedroom chair, whitewashed and chintz-squabbed.

the garden to solve the problem. New floorboards were laid on the diagonal to make the area appear more spacious. Having floorboards running at right angles from wall to wall across the room would have increased the sense of confinement, and running them parallel to the length of the room would have emphasized the uncomfortable, tunnel-like feeling of the space.

Panelling was installed around the room, made of MDF (medium-density fibreboard) panels, each laser-cut with a Gothic arch, inspired by the clerestory of the next-door church of Saint Laurence (fame at last!).

Creating a light space

It is difficult to escape a feeling of claustrophobia in a triangular room, but there are several tricks to reassure the eye. Most importantly – maximize light! Consider roof lights, whether as flat, swivelling, velux-type, or as raised dormers with their own roofs. Obviously the visual impact on the exterior of the building must be considered with either option.

The next thing to address is the inherent problem of too many dark, sharply angular corners. It's often better to 'waste' a square foot or so of floor space at floor level in a triangular room. Installing a false, dado-height wall will provide a much-needed vertical surface and flattening off floor-level corners around the space is one of the most efficient ways of making an attic appear much more spacious and room-like.

To create a feeling of brightness, freshness and light throughout this room, all the woodwork, including both new and old beams, was painted in a soft off-white.

Everything else was painted a pale mint green – an ideal colour for reflecting light and bringing a feeling of the outside indoors.

As a passionate gardener, I thought an element of pretty floral fabric would lift the scheme and introduce a note of delicate femininity. Although Sarah very much approved the idea of chintz in bedrooms, she was keen to repress the floral for office hours. As a compromise, I decided to use chintz as the lining for a reversible linen throw and as a panel on the blinds, so that it was revealed only when the blinds were closed. Our one indulgence was to cover the modern office chair in pretty floral fabric.

Lighting

When properly treated, there's no reason why an attic room cannot, in fact, be an exciting and enticing area and lighting can be invaluable in achieving this goal. Recessed spotlights are obviously impossible in an area where the roof is immediately on the other side of the ceiling. But there's no reason why the principle of recessed lighting cannot be reversed by installing floor lights; beams of light travelling upwards can make a dramatic statement in a room with sloping walls. This is particularly true if the lighting has been conceived to present a feeling of rhythm by illuminating equally spaced areas on either side of the room or, as here, between equally spaced beams.

As Sarah liked this idea and was keen to include interesting and exciting lighting solutions, I specified a series of floor lights to uplight the beams, as well as

right Disguising doors as walls is a straightforward and traditional designer's trick to ensure a rational integrity of wall finishes within a design scheme.

back-lit glass panels set into the floor on which glass vessels could be displayed.

Sarah's attic had enough head height for a modern, halogen-spot, tensioned-wire track, which I felt made an interesting modern statement next to the softness of the old beams. As with floor lamps, table lamps on low tables can be used to create deliberately placed patches or spills of light. In this case, tungsten lighting, as in conventional bulbs, can provide a golden, rather apricot glow to a space, which is ideal for creating cosy, grown-up illumination during the evening.

Decent task lighting for the office incarnation was provided by high-tension wires carrying low-voltage halogen spotlights.

Designing a dual-purpose space

Designing rooms that have to accommodate two functions is not the easiest brief, but, of course, when you get it right – the rewards are magnificent. You have achieved that wondrous goal: two rooms in one.

The most straightforward and necessary thing is to make sure you allow yourself a decent budget. Think in terms of the budget you would normally allow for two rooms to give yourself access to seriously clever storage solutions, which will convert a space from one use to another at the turn of a handle or the flick of a switch.

If the transformation is effected every day, make sure the design solutions are durable enough; tough surfaces, cleanable finishes and heavy-duty fittings are essential if the space is to work well and continue looking good. In this case, Sarah and I worked closely together to

design a personalized layout for the working area, making sure that everything had been catered for and that nothing essential was overlooked.

Since the majority of the scheme leaned towards the romantic, the office elements were kept contemporary, sleek and business-like. As a final finishing touch, I commissioned local artist, Paul Kessling to paint views that Sarah loved. His work in Chinese inks, while representational, is nevertheless completely modern – a perfect balance that summed up the scheme.

right A panel of toughened, opaque glass, lit from below, creates an unusual, bespoke display for coloured glass.

A LOOK AT THE DETAILS

 Luckily Sarah was no clutter queen so her orderly approach to her desk begged for quite grown-up, minimalist styling. Less tidy workers might find sleeping in the office a far from restful experience!

 Head height was at a premium so the beams supporting the roof had to be reinvented. Whilst we were at it, I installed arched, diagonal beams to bring more excitement to the long view of the space.

 An ergonomically-designed, bentwood office chair would ensure Sarah avoided back or neck strain. As a witty aside, we decided to cover it in a traditional floral fabric rather than the usual office hessian.

 A traditional floral fabric featured heavily in the bedroom incarnation, but could be discreetly tidied away during the day by reversing throws and cushions to reveal a plain linen lining.

 To indulge Sarah's love of strong curvaceous shapes, a continuous dado rail below the internal pitch of the roof received panels laser-cut with a delicate Gothic arch, inspired by the next-door church.

 There are only a handful of solutions for curtaining a window on a sloped wall, and since Sarah wanted to avoid anything too fussy, a crisp linen blind with a chintz panel seemed the obvious solution.

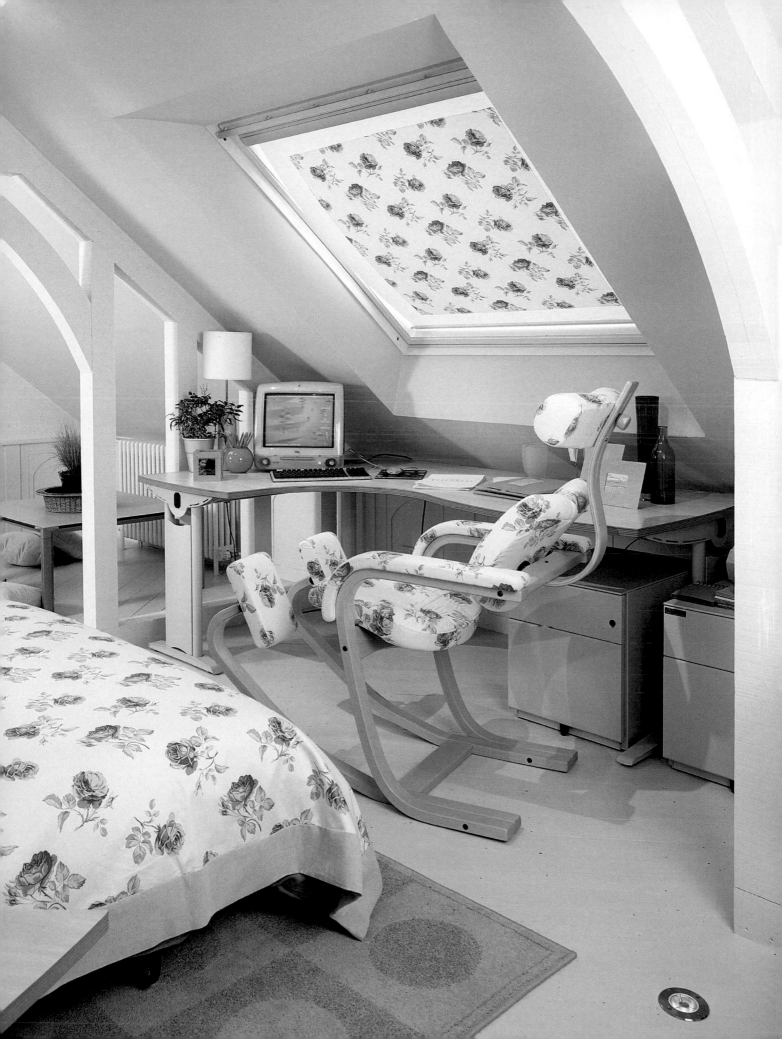

insideout
BATHROOMS

THE BATHROOM SPACE

A few years ago, a survey asked which was the most important, most personal space in the house. A huge percentage of respondents opted for the bathroom. In our busy, responsible lives it seems that the room with the lock is the one in which we feel most at home. There's so much about the bathroom that appeals – for a start every sense is catered for – sight, touch, smell and sound. Clever retailers over the past few years have built empires based on our quest for gorgeous smelling, self-indulgent bathtime treats. It's all a far cry from the traditional British bathroom of ten years ago, with its mouldy grouting, smelly shower curtain and, heaven help us, the avocado loo!

Having a bathroom at home should be a constant source of joy to us – instead, for many, it's a rather dismissed fact of life. Even the Romans, imperial organizers of genius and originators of contemporary plumbing, rarely had their own bathrooms, preferring instead to socialize at the bathhouse. Rooms designated specifically for bathing were rare until well into the 19th century and only became universally available in really quite recent history.

As a society, our ideas on cleanliness are constantly

opposite The loft-living dream extends even into the exposed brick bathroom...

right ...whereas the rural retreat offers a design scheme that fuses bathroom with dovecote.

changing. It's bizarre, in today's hygiene-conscious times, to discover that, rather than being next to godliness, cleanliness was considered hugely unhealthy by the good people of the medieval period. They believed that the gruesome 'crust' of grime – and God knows what else – that encased their bodies kept diseases out and held goodness in. Of course, although disgusting, there's something in this; one can be over-pasteurized and, to build up immunity, our bodies need a little controlled practice with the bugs they have to defend us against. Not that I am in any way promoting BO, do understand. Once society decided to discourage the fundamentally antisocial practice of smelling bad, bathing became a symbol of wealth, with associations of luxury and indulgence that have never really left it.

Now, of course, we all have access to fresh, clean bathing water and, by extension, a degree of ownership, whatever our true circumstances, in the luxurious connotations of the bathtime traditions.

But think back one hundred years to the onerous task of filling by hand a tin bath placed in front of the fire, or the weekly reliance on visits to the bathhouse – an experience, I'm sure, that was every bit as social as in Roman times. Remember, too, the extraordinarily complicated rituals associated with bathing in ancient times. The Egyptians, Greeks, Romans and Japanese all saw bathing in quasi-religious terms, above and beyond the more prosaic need to keep clean and not offend those around you with a cloud of odour.

Design considerations

As our lives become more and more congested, we see the bathroom as having to fulfil two separate roles. At night when we're very much on 'our time', the bathroom is a retreat, a cocoon in which the cares of the day can be soaked away in a comforting sea of rich-smelling lather by candlelight. Whereas in the mornings, when time is at a premium and there's an entire family to wash and prepare to face the day, speed and convenience prevail.

Technology

Fitting out a bathroom is an expensive business, even at the most basic level. Because it has become such a psychologically important space for us, we are prepared to spend more and more money on raising the bathroom to the status of a real 'treat' area.

Technology continues to advance, offering us the benefits of remote control showers, timed taps, micro-touch thermostats and underfloor heating. But it's often

the basics that give pleasure: the gorgeous smells of scented unguents enjoyed by candlelight, the serene drip, drip, drip of the tap.

Building regulations

There are some very basic building regulations to bear in mind when designing a bathroom; which you should never forget if you want to change the layout of an existing bathroom. First, you should be aware of where the water waste pipes are; they're easy to spot by looking outside – they are the thicker pipes. Moving the fittings too far from this soil stack will cause all sorts of problems, because you'll need metres of pipework to take used water from the bath or loo to the existing pipework. This is particularly difficult if the pipe needs to cross a doorway – stepping over a large pipe to get into the bathroom is hardly ideal. One solution would be to raise the floor level throughout the area to create a cavity that will take all the gubbins required.

Another important issue is weight. Modern acrylic or rolled steel baths weigh very little; traditional roll top cast iron baths weigh a ton (almost literally). But whatever the style of bath, when filled with water and you, you're talking about something with a very high point-loading. So, even if you can solve the plumbing issues of moving the bath to the centre of the room, make sure that your builder contacts a structural engineer who is happy the floor can take the strain.

Bath or shower?

As a nation, we have recently fallen in love with showering. As a means of washing, we used to dismiss the shower as an American gimmick but now, with crowded mornings and more deadlines than you can shake a stick at, the idea of a few minutes in an invigorating jet of water makes sense.

With showers, always remember that to achieve that stream of champagne-bubble soft water, you'll need quite high water pressure. Many British homes are not equipped to cope with levels of pressure required, so it's a good idea to have the whole water system appraised and improved. Pumps can help, but you should also bear in mind the quantities of hot water you'll be swallowing up in your quest for the perfect shower.

Urban metropolitan areas tend to have very hard water. Hard water and the limescale deposits it leaves behind are the enemies of the bathroom. It's not just

left A modern solution that capitalizes on the view through to the roof garden.

that it looks awful; it clogs up the fine holes on the showerhead and reduces the efficiency of taps like clogged arteries. A water softener is a good investment to prolong the life of your snazzy bathroom fittings.

Bathroom style

As far as the look of bathrooms go – the world is your oyster. There are, of course, a few practical constraints. Never forget to include plenty of storage, for instance, but, by and large, it's an area where you can really let your hair down. There's been a pronounced recent trend for fantasy decoration in bathrooms, with schemes that revive the glories of ancient Egypt, Pompeii or 18th century France.

There is, it has to be said, a particularly glamorous history to bathing, and many of us are seduced by the idea of becoming Cleopatra at bathtime. Unfortunately, the ancient reality was probably something of a smelly disappointment – my dear, the residue of all that asses' milk!

Bathrooms can certainly take emphatically rich design statements and, if one bears in mind that, as a room, the bathroom is the closest thing we've got to an escape pod, don't feel bullied into a particular style. Allow yourself the indulgence of being expressive – if you want to forget the mundanities of everyday life, or if you want to create the atmosphere of a New York loft in a Surrey semi – then do it. It really is up to you.

inside BATHROOM SANCTUARY

above Light floods into the ultimate in bathroom luxury – a room that celebrates space.

opposite Annexing a larger room for the bathroom meant that storage had to be found for Paul's and Sarah's clothes so that the bedroom could house the bed and nothing else.

SITING YOUR BATHROOM

Think about what you want from your bathroom, then consider whether its current location best fulfils your desires. If you can't escape the whine of traffic, or the constant whoosh of overhead aircraft, consider fighting fire with fire by introducing constant, gentle noise that gives pleasure. Wind chimes or an internal water feature can create a tranquil sound bubble that forces external noise to stay outside, while encouraging the ear to register only more peaceful sounds.

When I saw Sarah and Paul's house, my first reaction was to swap their existing bedroom at the noisy front of the house for a smaller space overlooking the back garden. This would allow for a better night's sleep and give room for a luxuriously un-cramped bathroom and dressing-room layout that would meet their criteria.

This sort of work needs expert advice, both in regard to moving the plumbing, and in case you decide to remove walls or introduce partitions. In this case, I gave instructions for a huge doorway to be built between bedroom and bathroom and then, following structural briefings, a raised floor in the bathroom to allow for essential services such as waste water outlets. It also created the potential to include invisible structural beams to bear the weight of a centrally placed bath.

Building rules

Never forget when designing a bathroom that a bath full of water weighs an enormous amount. In an old Victorian terrace, such as Sarah's and Paul's, the floorboards in the middle of the room are likely to be

The Brief

To create an inner sanctum of a bathroom that could accommodate two busy, rushed consultants when they prepared for the day first thing in the morning, and then needed soothing last thing at night. Twin basins were a must, as was a powerful shower. Plenty of storage space was needed, including a place to hang clothes; the area would have to fulfil the role of dressing room as well.

Their Requirements

Pale blonde timber and natural materials in abundance, although heavy theming in the direction of Scandinavian design, Feng Shui, or faux-Japanese style was to be avoided at all costs. Light had to be maximized and the area as a whole should feel contemporary without brutal or faddish detailing. Above all things – tranquillity and calm. The room overlooked one of Islington's busiest roads, so anything that could segregate the room from its urban context should be considered. Low-level lighting for luxury bathing would have to co-exist with clear, bright task lighting for first thing on a winter's morning.

The Materials

Cool, pale-coloured natural materials were required wherever possible. Marmorina (marble-dust, polished plaster), fennel-coloured linoleum, and blonde plywood a-plenty were offset against brushed stainless steel, acid-etched glass and cobbles.

unequal to the job. Originally, I toyed with the idea of a wooden bath. I had seen wooden, bowl-shaped basins that would be ideal for the look I had in mind, but I felt that the wooden baths on offer looked like oversized salad bowls. So, in the end, I opted for a large acrylic bath, around which a wooden surround could be built. This I designed in plywood, laminating sheet after sheet to achieve a striped sandwich of end grain.

Ground-floor bathrooms can accommodate just about anything, regardless of weight but, since most us have baths upstairs, one has to be mindful of, for instance, stone or marble floors placing too much stress on the joists. If the natural look is important to you, but the floorboards simply aren't up to it, there are patterned, cushioned vinyls available that are credible facsimiles of a range of timbers, stones, marbles or granites.

Creating a focal point

As with any space, a bathroom needs a focal point. Since most of the bathroom furniture cannot be moved

left Much was made of strong, linear architectural statements in the scheme; using defined horizontals to knit the space together with pronounced verticals to add height.

around like a three-piece suite in a living room, consider carefully the views from bath, shower or loo, making a point of placing objects where they can be properly appreciated and enjoyed. A bold colour statement often draws the eye successfully to a wall you might want to make a fuss of. Older houses might have a chimney-breast that could provide the opportunity for placing pillar candles on a sill with cobbles or shells. An interestingly framed mirror or art piece can be called upon to bring detail to an otherwise unadorned wall. And never forget that windowsills or shelves can be used to display interesting objects, as well as offering easy-to-reach storage for bathtime necessities.

Less aesthetic bath products are the bane of every parent's bathtime. Bath toys should be stored in receptacles that have a close relationship with the overall scheme. Although be careful of using baskets or cloth-covered storage bins since they can be prone to rot in bathrooms that don't have adequate ventilation.

I wanted the bath to be raised on steel legs, so that the whole structure didn't dominate the room; I then used panels of mirror to disguise the unlovely workings such as pipes, wastes and pumps. Around the mirror, I created a top-lit trough that was filled with pebbles

which, when reflected in the mirror, appeared to stretch into infinity.

For the perimeter of the space, I commissioned Californian Closets, cupboard makers to the stars, to lay out a series of storage solutions behind etched glass doors. Similar doors disguised the lavatory and shower so that the bath became the main feature, drawing the eye to the centre of the room and celebrating the luxury of space around it.

On either side of the chimney-breast, plywood was used to form work surfaces upon which wooden basins were mounted. To increase the feeling of height, long narrow slots of mirror above each basin reflected space and light, as well as allowing for precision shaving.

Disguising unsightly objects

Bathrooms are a minefield of pipes. Rooms that were not originally intended to house baths, loos, basins or showers often require service pipes to be run across walls or floors. If you have no alternatives and no possibility of absorbing pipework beneath the floor, or in wall cavities, you will need to address the question of whether you are happy to see distracting pipework upstaging your swanky new bath, or whether you are going to box the pipes in.

If you are the boxing kind, my advice is to be as architectural as possible. Try to integrate the boxing into a storage unit, or allow it to be read as an architectural feature, such as a skirting board or door frame. Don't be frightened to make boxing bigger than it needs to be, or indeed, to balance the boxing-in of one side of the bath with dummy boxing of the same proportions elsewhere,

right The pale colours and natural finishes of the room were offset against the dark, natural slate tiling used in the shower enclosure and Andy Goldsworthy's slate illustration, to add an exciting dissonance to the scheme.

if that's what it takes to achieve symmetry. Above all, however, remember that boxing needs to be accessible.

If, perish the thought, your plumbing goes into meltdown, your plumber will need access to the pipes, so easily removable sections, although more complicated to construct, will be more sensible in the long run. At the window, acid-etched glass shutters blocked the view into the bathroom from the bus stop on the opposite side of the street.

Flooring

I chose linoleum for the floor. Few people realize it's a natural material based largely on linseed oil and wood waste. It's a lot less slippery than most other floor coverings and is naturally antiseptic, which was good with a baby on the way. I also liked the fact that, as a sheet material, it would provide a seamless finish that could reflect the light from the two street-facing windows. The chosen colour, a pale fennel green, worked well with the putty coloured walls and the well-behaved, blonde tones of the plywood.

Finishing touches

The bathroom cried out for a suitably contemplative art piece in which one could lose oneself during a long soak. The landscape artist, Andy Goldsworthy, provided the perfect solution and, thanks to the art website, 'Eyestorm', which specializes in photographic art pieces, Paul and Sarah chose a framed print of one of Andy's slate illustrations. A nice back-reference to the slate used to tile the shower enclosure.

right Wooden basins were the ideal solution in a bathroom which celebrates natural materials. Bathroom decoration has taken on many new and exciting finishes to create excitingly different spaces.

For people with busy lives, the bathroom is extremely important and Paul and Sarah quickly became accustomed to the sensual assault offered by their new bathroom. It really was the sort of bathroom that one would need at least two chocolate flakes to truly enjoy!

A LOOK AT THE DETAILS

Time was when basins came in steel or acrylic – period. Now the choice encompasses glass, slate, copper, stone or, as here, wood. Basins make a soft statement in a bathroom and can augment the architectural scheme when mounted on a timber plinth or shelf.

This tall, heated rail combines bathroom heating with warm towel storage. Modern towel rails can make an elegant statement and those with a refined ladder design, as here, create a narrow vertical emphasis, which makes the ceiling appear higher.

Make the most of the fact that the bath dominates the bathroom. Here, the surround doesn't meet the floor, but a mirrored plinth, set back from the face of the surround, hides pipework and reflects the floor to infinity, so the bath seems to float above a sea of cobbles.

The view from the window was of nothing more glamorous than a bus stop and eternal ribbons of traffic, so we used swivelling acid-etched glass shutters in painted timber frames to filter out the evidence of urban living while softening the daylight.

Discretely styled taps and mixer are mounted on a low plywood wall that accommodates the pipe work. The wall creates a discrete feeling of enclosure in the bath and acts rather like the headboard of a bed. It also offers a convenient place to put your chocolate flake!

Even modernists need somewhere to light candles. A kinetic sculpture, inspired by the work of Alexandra Calder, was commissioned to include little sleeves for tea-lights that ensured a soft, romantic ambience for bathing *à deux*.

insideout
LIVING ROOMS

above The Gothic tradition reborn for a new age. Natural materials and rich finishes combine to create a space packed with interest and detail. Note the table lamp, powered by a floor socket behind the sofa, to bring light into the middle of the room.

THE LIVING ROOM THEN

To me, it's very illuminating that, as a generation, we occupy 'living rooms'. Our grandparents were so much more specific about naming their reception rooms; there were 'sitting rooms', 'drawing rooms', 'morning rooms' and 'breakfast rooms' – all given a name, a purpose and a different way of decorating. Our forebears went further and claimed ownership of 'parlours', 'games rooms', 'withdrawing rooms' and the like.

For us, the fact that most of the ground floor of our houses has been christened a 'living' area denotes our informality. Bizarrely, there is a direct parallel with the ultra-formal lifestyle of the 17th and 18th centuries, where the main reception rooms were often known simply by the colour of their decorative schemes since their function was decided on an impromptu hour-by-hour basis. Servants would move tables for dining from one room to another at the whim of the master or mistress. Most rooms would have everything required for 'sitting' and, since much of the day was gender-segregated, a 'parlour' (a very female space), could be created anywhere, while a 'games room' (where the boys hung out) required a portable card table and little else.

right Colour has here been used as a restrained treat. Oatmeal rules ok! bringing form to the fore.

THE LIVING ROOM NOW

The biggest difference between then and now is, of course, square footage. An organic, peripatetic way of living, as enjoyed by the Regency buck, relied on suite after suite of rooms. For us, space is at a premium, so the fact that we live in living rooms denotes just how many daily activities we expect to pursue in the one space. Having said that, we now live in a more informal way; if there is to be a small element of formality in our lives, it will nearly always happen in either the dining room or the living room. Both are public spaces and, as such, might still reflect a vestigial need to display wealth or position. The living room mantelshelf always seems to attract the 'best possessions': the heirlooms, the wedding presents, and it is the place where invitations and family photographs take root. Most of us fight hard to hang on to the concept of a fireplace, which is odd in the age of central heating. The fire is no longer the focus of the space, because nine times out of ten, we'd rather spend the evening watching the flickering blue light of the television than the apricot flicker of flames.

DESIGN CONSIDERATIONS

So, what is the best way of decorating a living room? I have always favoured a softly modern approach that stops well short of pristine, but is nevertheless stylish.

Who are you designing for?

As the size of our homes shrinks, the more activities have to be squeezed into the living room, and the more family members expect a corner for themselves. The living room is often the most difficult room to keep tidy and, therefore, for many people, the most difficult to design. Most people who have committed themselves to modernist or minimalist room schemes, which depend on contrived furniture arrangements, pale colours and an absence of clutter, often regret the decision within an hour of the children returning from school. The way the living room works, and ultimately the way the living room looks, will always have to be a compromise that takes account of all the needs of all its potential users.

Our approach to colour is, without doubt, benefiting from increased confidence. Strong colours sell well these

left The fireplace has been well and truly celebrated in this living room, and the architectural fire screen flags up the cosy message that this is a working fire.

days and they are often to be found in living rooms. At its most simplistic, a decent, emphatic colour scheme should be considered in terms of balance, that is, colour on the walls and neutral everything else, or neutral walls and colour on the furniture. But the trend is definitely for more multi-layered colour schemes, offsetting large blocks of plain colour by using accents of coordinating objects in paler or stronger shades.

Personally, I've found that confident colour schemes are best conceived as flavours. Imagine each shade has a specific taste; red could be tomato soup or, if further towards the blue end of the spectrum, raspberry. Savour these flavours, roll them around your tongue for a while and then start to decide what flavours you can add to provide depth. Tomatoes, for example, have a sweetness that can be enlivened with black pepper, or herbs such as blue-hued basil. Raspberries are piquant and quite sharp and, as such, suit pastry or cream as a more neutral antidote. Assemble your colour palette as you would culinary ingredients; ascribe a flavour to each and you'll find colour easier to understand by far.

Style

A durable colour palette is essential. Richer, warmer colours not only wear well, they also create an inviting, relaxing atmosphere. Flexible seating helps: a series of

right Detailed leading in this new French door lends an interesting twist to traditional glazing patterns.

above Indulgent
textures always excite.

right Order your clutter
for artistic effect.

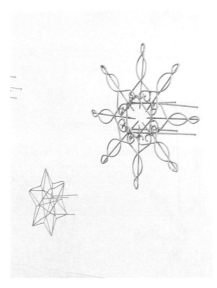

above Architecture is celebrated by a neutral colour
scheme.

left A sculptural wall solution that casts shadows and
reflects light. The ultimate 3-D wallpaper.

smaller furniture groups allows for several different activities (television, homework, reading etc.) in the way that one gigantic sofa at the end of the room doesn't. An inbuilt but easily controlled element of clutter means that dropped Sunday papers or discarded toys don't stick out like sore thumbs. And a series of different lighting scenarios, from bright overhead light for tasks, to smoochy, moody table lamps for relaxation, allows the space to reincarnate through the day from a 'family' to an 'adult' area. Above all, and I suppose all of the above requirements highlight the same issue: the living room must be comfortable.

Before finalizing a scheme, sit down and make sure that you have provided the space and appropriate facilities for everyone likely to be using the room. Think about 'zones'; for example, for television watching (or should I say worshipping?), reading, computers or hobbies. Even relatively small rooms can take a series of furniture scenarios in which each member of the family can pursue their own activities.

inside  MODERN CLASSICS

UPDATING A CLASSIC

If you own a period house you may decide that you would like to update its style rather than restore it to its former glory by replacing all its original features. This can work extremely well if handled sensitively. Updating a classic – it's a question of balancing what you want with what the room has always been. The most fundamental advice I can give is to dissuade iconoclastic modernists from moving into homes rich in period detail and, likewise, I suggest that cluttered traditionalists shouldn't try to live in glass cubes.

This house was exceptional – one of the finest in Northampton. Gracefully restrained as only Regency houses can be, its style and period would have to be reflected in the scheme. For this design, Catherine's principal request was for a scheme that mingled old

The Brief

An adult haven that allowed for glamorous evening dinner parties, or for less formal easy-going afternoons, that would suit 10-year-old daughter, Flora, who is profoundly autistic. This area was to be very much for her, Catherine, Jim and their son, Kyle, to relax in.

Their Requirements

They felt an easy-going respect for the existing architecture, but were happy for me to improve the proportions of the room by removing extraneous, inappropriate details.

Everything new had to coordinate with the age and style of the house, while bringing the room very much up-to-date. Texture was important, as was comfort, but for Jim and Catherine, style was to be king. Tranquillity and relaxation were the order of the day.

The Materials

The original broad floorboards were left untouched and their honey tones worked well with the jewel-coloured walls. Pale neutral shades of driftwood and copper created an interesting, sculptural palette of accent colours and textures.

right Easy-going and contemporary, the furniture seems to have grown organically into its position. Note the interplay of rounded natural forms and square sculptural solids.

and new and that remained stimulating and textural. Jim wanted something comfortable (and, of course, everything that Catherine wanted too!).

First things first meant removing a lot of large-patterned 1980s wallpaper as well as the meanly inappropriate architectural elements, such as the recently installed fireplaces, picture rails and architraves. In addition, the window facing the garden cried out to be reborn as a French door, giving access to the outside.

The fireplaces were an important architectural feature of the space, but were spoiled by the flimsy pine surrounds that Jim and Catherine had inherited with the house. I opted for impressive French-style stone overmantels with simple, integrated mouldings that would act as a mantelpiece.

In the living room, the motto '*Sine Baccho et Cerere friget Venus*' was carved by hand into the stone. It's a favourite quote of mine from the Roman author, Terence, and, loosely translated, it means: 'without wine and food, love grows cold'.

The contemporary touches

For me, creating a balance, a fusion between the best of the old and the new, is akin to Arthur's quest for the Holy Grail. As a nation, we have one foot in the past and the other in the present, and there's no sense in denying it. Designers and architects of the 20th century saw the future as a place to escape to, and unleashed acres of concrete rabbit hutches onto an unsuspecting planet. In doing so, they forgot the most important thing – the present.

The contemporary of today is the antique of tomorrow in the same way that, two hundred and fifty years ago, Chippendale chairs were scary modern statements. So my advice is not to focus too heavily on chronology – don't become too fixated on when

something was made, simply evaluate it on its aesthetic merit. Look for a unity in the objects in a room, a linking colour, texture, form or proportion. Never close your mind to unusual and surprising combinations and don't be afraid of putting Georgian next to George Davis. And always remember that monetary value is a notion that is irrelevant to whether or not you like something, or whether or not it works in the room.

The general feel of the scheme was to be grand without being overbearing. The fireplaces – powerful statements in stone – were simple and modern, while the rich red walls, in a shade beloved by the original Georgian builders of the house, were welcoming and cosy. The copper light fittings and a wealth of finishing touches added contemporary touches to the design.

In the dining area, the coordinating fire surround, as in the living room, broke up the rich red walls.

The simple, almost rustic, tabletop and sculptural steel chairs lent a feeling of almost monastic tranquillity to this end of the room. I had commissioned these steel-framed dining chairs for their cheeky resemblance to directors' chairs (something of an obsession in the 1970s) but, in the living room, there were large, comfortable sofas with a more blocky silhouette.

Colour
It was obvious that these high-ceilinged rooms could take a rich, adventurous colour, which was why I opted for red. In my experience, red emulsion gives a flat, rather dowdy finish, so I designed a paint effect that began with a rather scary flamingo pink as a base coat, on top of which a rich red, morocco-leather-coloured glaze was close-stippled to allow the oomph of the pink to shine through. The effect was warm and surprisingly modern.

far right top Even the lighting solutions felt sculptural. Grouping lamps as a quasi still life called to mind ancient British standing stones. Remember to use low-wattage bulbs unless you want the effect to look like a department store.

far right bottom The contemporary coffee table with its curved, almost pebble-like outline, create a perfect centre point to the squarely rugged outlines of the sofa and chair.

right Even the radiator cabinet offered potential for integrating into the scheme.

One of the most important things to remember about using strong shades – such as this red – is to maintain balance by offsetting strength with as much neutrality as possible. In this scheme, I combined coarse red linen on the dining chairs with the soft, stone-coloured suiting that was used to upholster the sofa and chairs, to create a tactile and highly visual haven.

Incorporating art into your scheme

We are, I believe, a nation of closet art lovers. Just about everyone has at least one postcard of a favourite painting somewhere in the house, but most of us can't claim to own an original, which is a surprise considering how accessible art actually is.

I loved the idea of indulging Catherine's and Jim's artistic streak and using it to bring the bold red walls alive with a series of sculptural statements. Art was to play an important part in the grand design. I wanted to include some of Barbara Hepworth's powerfully abstracted evocations of the rugged Celtic landscape. Hepworth's use of mass and form continues to inspire product designers today, so I assembled accessories from lamp bases to vases that were derivative of her work.

Applied art was all well and good, but I felt it would be neglectful not to include an original art piece. I took Catherine and Jim to the Degree Show at the Camberwell School of Art, my old college, to shop for art from the work displayed by final year students. My clients fell in love with a highly textural piece made from linked wire that had a distinctly knitted feel to it. Convenient really, because my *pièce de résistance* within the scheme were the machine-knitted curtains that I had evolved with Monarch Textiles.

A LOOK AT THE DETAILS

Copper elements, as in this fire screen, reflect the light. Copper is a soothing metallic finish that is not as vulgar as gold, or as clinical as steel. Wrought ironwork, at its most simple, played an important role in the scheme.

The unusual textures of this modern mirror, based on a Regency starburst, but executed in Cornish driftwood, bring an element of outdoors into the scheme. The informal nature of 'found' driftwood contrasts well with the dressed stone of the fire surround.

Simple, blocky furniture shapes work extremely well in Georgian interiors. The outlines of upholstered furniture, as well as storage units such as these, were deliberately understated for maximum impact.

Making a strong statement with the central ceiling light helps to distribute interest evenly around the room. The opaque glass and brushed copper fittings coordinated with finishes elsewhere in the room.

The knitted fabrics used for curtains hang beautifully and allow a gentle tease of light into the room. For winter evenings, they exude the same kind of cosy warmth as a favourite jumper.

The contemporary coffee table, with its curvaceous, almost pebble-like outline, creates a perfect counterpoint to the squarely rugged outlines of the sofa and chair.

inside GRAND LIVING

above The dining room: feminine and sociable with a bold palette of ivory and peacock enlivened with black.

CREATING ORDER

There are those that would take the clutter of the nation and ignite a great bonfire in Trafalgar Square.

But as far as I can see, life without clutter would be impossible for most of us, particularly in today's society for those with families and/or hectic lifestyles. Having said that, however, one should at least try to bring order out of chaos, and re-tailor cluttered spaces strewn with objects and discordant architectural details into more austerely classical spaces.

Removing large, cluttering features from a room will give it a feeling of more space instantly, so here I decided to remove the fire surrounds and replace them with mantelpieces a good few centimetres lower than normal. Vina also had in place large, ungainly sofas, which dwarfed the room and which would have to be replaced with more appropriately sized seating. The less cluttered effect that I strived for was well and truly rammed home by placing large, over-scaled mirrors above each fireplace to reflect light and space.

The Brief

To create a glamorous, classically elegant space that belied the reality of Kingston. The living room should be ideal for snuggling, but sophisticated and beautifully detailed. The essentially small rooms should feel twice the size once the scheme was complete.

Her Requirements

It was obvious from her tearsheet presentation that Vina was drawn to glamour like a moth to a flame.

Lapis lazuli bowls, malachite, mementos of Egypt and reproductions of the *femmes fatales* painted by the Viennese artist, Gustav Klimt, and celebrated in Art Nouveau culture. Above all of this was a fascination for the iridescent beauty of the peacock feather. Vina wanted all that is elegant and to fuse it together to create a feminine environment. Classical references were to be encouraged but not over-indulged, while richness and luxury were to be the keynotes of the finishing touches. The room should be soft and grown up like an *haute couture* sari, playing on traditions from a variety of cultures. The sort of environment a great hostess or society Grande Dame might take for granted, but one that would not overpower a 21st century career girl.

The Materials

There was no doubt that Vina was a glamour puss; gold, malachite, rich materials, detailed embroidered patterns in shades of blue-green and green-blue.

Creating space

In Vina's house, architecturally-speaking, the rooms felt low and undistinguished, with a series of nooks, crannies and ceiling beams that fractured any sense of rhythm or serenity. My first instinct was to create rhythm out of chaos by using carefully laid out, slender columns, which I felt would not only harmonize the spaces but also increase the feeling of height.

It's one of the oldest tricks in the book to use as many verticals as possible in a low-ceilinged room to fool the eye into thinking the walls are taller. So specially-commissioned plaster mouldings, cornices, columns, niches and brackets were all installed, while the architectural anomalies around the chimney-breasts were panelled over to accommodate commodious storage spaces. The dividing screen wall was then pierced with two symmetrical apertures to provide illuminated display spaces.

above An elegant, embroidered peacock feather.

Using accents and details

Interior design is all about proportions, relationships and, ultimately, balance. Painting a room a pale colour

far right Black lacquer as the ultimate mascara-dark accent statement.

right Feminine styling, floral and light.

opposite The richness of peacock silk offset by ivory.

above Real peacock feathers turn a lampshade into an Ascot hat.

in its entirety rather loses the point of the pale colour – it's a bit like gorging on pasta. Introducing an element of the piquant – the opposite – the dark side in the scheme, provides the opportunity to redefine the space in more balanced terms.

Committing yourself to architectural accents is a bold step so the wary should start on the nursery slopes with moveable (and removable) accessories. The basic bones were taking shape – the odd, classically inspired detail beside more clean-cut, modern architectural elements.

A love of peacocks and the iridescent colours of their feathers had come out strongly in the tearsheet, so I decided to use these strong tones as an accent in an essentially all-ivory space.

Ivory and peacock is an unusual combination, but it's one that I consider immediately redolent of glamorous sophistication. Since the scheme was to be all about Vina's glamorous side, we visited a sari shop where I took inspiration from the delicacy of Indian embroidery and the richness of sari silk.

For the floor, I found a new take on traditional classic parquet; bamboo laid in intricate patterns, which is a durable, light coloured and highly decorative surface.

The furniture

When choosing furniture for your living room, remember to think practically as well as visually. There's no point in having a sleek, glamorous sofa if it's unbearably uncomfortable and you end up covering it in cushions so that you can sit on it. Vina's ideal evening was to cuddle up on a soft, deep sofa. I loved this brief, so I designed a large *chaise longue* in the form of a sofa bed that was unusually deep in the seat – for an increased cuddle-up factor – but which also had elegant, classically inspired lines.

A matching companion seat and pouffe were also made, and the whole suite was to be upholstered in rich peacock-coloured silk that was machine embroidered with randomly placed, peacock-feather motifs in iridescent metallic threads. The same motif found its way on to ivory silk curtains, which had box pleats lined in the peacock silk of the furniture.

The secret to using an accent successfully is to make sure that it is just that, an accent. Accents should be used sparingly and in a subtle way. The rich turquoise tones of traditional bath aqua glassware offered the perfect translucent accent and the bespoke table lamps with peacock-blue silk shades reflected a sophisticated, clean light around both rooms.

The final touch was gilding. Vina professed a love of gold leaf, but I felt that traditional yellow gold would be an additional colour that we could do without, not least because it would unbalance the scheme. So white gold leaf, a rare and frankly exotic oddity, was used in the niches and around the apertures to elevate the glam factor to scale 8.

A LOOK AT THE DETAILS

 Since space was at a premium, placing lamps in the niches that were integrated with the panelling meant that the floor area need not be cluttered up with occasional tables bearing lamp bases.

 Glossy ebony next to soft peacock silk, a perfectly matched marriage of opposites that brought life and vigour to the principally ivory-toned space.

 The dizzyingly fractured architectural space needed light management and a sense of rhythm and order, which was imposed using the slender, regularly spaced columns.

 Room for a little indulgence. Ornately carved ornamental mirrors with bath aqua hand-blown vessels supported on extravagantly moulded corbel brackets – a touch of *fin de siècle grand luxe*.

 White gold leaf has none of the sickly yellow connotations of its golden cousin, but is warmer than silver leaf, which can feel cold and chilly. A pale blue was used behind the leaf to add depth and interest.

 Intricately embroidered peacock feathers were scattered randomly over the upholstered furniture and curtains for a slightly surreal glamour.

inside A GOTHIC LIVING ROOM

above A rich, comfortable environment decorated with a sufficiency of simple, natural finishes to keep the scheme cool and effortlessly elegant.

DIVIDING A ROOM

Usually we want to tear down room divisions to create a larger, more open room. Sometimes, however, it makes sense to divide up a room instead.

The current obsession with open-plan living had resulted in the loss of division between Andy and Lizzie's sitting and dining rooms. Opening out rooms works extremely well in most situations, and can solve many problems, but open-plan rooms bring their own set of disadvantages. The idea of enjoying space is immensely appealing, but open-plan does mean that any noise created travels to other areas of the house. Open-plan arrangements, of course, also mean that there are no private spaces within the room.

For these clients, two rooms were most definitely better than one, as we needed to accommodate Andy and Lizzie's large television and its constant companion, Lizzie's Dad. So the dividing wall had to go back into the room to create a space where he could watch television without disturbing anyone else in the

right Honey-toned oak against jade green walls is a country house classic in decorating terms – almost as classic as jade brocade.

room, or *vice versa*. The room was L-shaped, so I decided to relegate the television to the smaller branch of the room, and suggested constructing a glazed screen and door to segregate the two spaces, so that the whole room still felt open, light and spacious.

What was left of the 'L' was to be a sophisticated, grown-up space – principally a living room for Andy and Lizzie to relax in, but with sufficient flexibility for it to be used for dining and entertaining.

The Brief

To create two rooms from one L-shaped space. In the larger area, a grown-up living room for reading, entertaining and listening to music. The smaller area was designated as a space in which Lizzie's Dad could watch the huge, all-singing, all-dancing television, without disturbing the grown-ups. I incorporated views of and access into the garden by lengthening the window openings to create French doors.

Andy and Lizzie added a very personal, very specific and, it has to be said, extraordinary element to the brief – a brightly coloured, resin figurine of a dragon.

Their Requirements

Andy and Lizzie had a very personal take on the Gothic style, emphasizing a romantic, fairy-tale element replete with dragons and mysticism. I, on the other hand, wanted to reincarnate the Gothic with a modernity borne of carefully editing out much of the extraneous ornament. The new room was to be serene and restrained, but comfortable and welcoming; related to the garden, but also cosily independent for fire-lit winter evenings.

The Materials

Mid-toned oak predominated, offset by pale, light-reflective stone flags. The rich jade wall colour carried through to the damask furnishing fabric. Accents of oiled steel worked well against the softness of ivory velvet.

left Although the effect is quite dense, the forms themselves are actually very simple: arches, circles and squares.

was used to frame a new stone fireplace. The elegant, elongated arches of the Early English Gothic (a quintessentially English phenomenon of the 13th century), suited our quest for simple, unornamented vertical forms perfectly.

Using colour

Cool colours reflect light so well and, for a small space with so much going on in it, a theme of jade and ivory was the perfect solution. Originally, Andy and Lizzie had envisaged the room in a warm, rich palette of reds and burnt golds, but I feel that those colours are more appropriate for a bedroom. Warm colours are great for creating a cosy inner sanctum, but for a multi-purpose living room like this one, with direct access to the garden via French doors, lighter colours would help to create a more congruous mood.

The pale stone floor, which was laid on the diagonal, matched the stone fire surround with its softened Gothic arch, resulting in a serene, uncluttered mood.

In this scheme, the style was essentially very masculine, so we needed to find a way to soften the effect. The choice of fabric is an important one in any design, but especially so when you want to moderate strong styling. Again, simplicity was the key, so a jade damask in the same shade as on the walls was used to cover the clean-lined sofa and modern dining chairs. The same fabric was used as a panel on the wall opposite the fireplace.

With its pronounced ecclesiastical connotations, damask may have seemed a cheeky choice for a modern

Fantasy styles

Never ever forget that your home is your own and it is most definitely entirely up to you how it looks. If you have a burning desire to live in a Moroccan boudoir or a Pompeiian atrium – then why waste time dreaming? Why not get on with it? Andy and Lizzie very much had the confidence and, by thunder, they had the theme. The look for this room was Gothic!

But I was very keen that it should be Gothic with one foot placed firmly in the present. I designed a variety of Gothic-inspired elements for the space, all the time reworking and refining familiar Gothic motifs, such as painted arches and pinnacles, until they were simplified to their basic essence. This is a very modernist concept, and this ethos came through clearly in the oak panelling, which incorporated storage and

Gothic living room. But its rich, shiny surface created a perfect counterpoint to Lizzie's preferred curtain choice – ivory velvet – to which I added the supreme luxury of ivory leather edging.

Gothic influences

One of the real inspirations for my scheme was the architect, George Pace, whose work I had seen at Llandaff Cathedral, near Cardiff. Pace trod a successful line between the 1950s modernism of his own era and the more venerable, ecclesiastical Gothic traditions. His work greatly influenced the decorative accessories that I had made to complement the scheme – stubby, pillar candle bases in oiled cut steel, table lamps to match and soft scatter cushions in a patchwork of contrasting green damasks.

The windows themselves, framing views of Diarmuid's Gothic-arched garden, needed something special to create a truly Gothic feel. I designed glazed panels to fit into oak doors that fused Gothic form with more than a sprinkle of Charles Rennie Mackintosh.

It would have been a bit of a job squeezing Andy's love of Judge Dredd comics into such a sophisticated scheme, and I felt that the work of the 18th century Italian artist, Giambattista Piranesi, had so much more in common with the overall mood. Andy agreed, so Piranesi won over the Incredible Hulk as framed fine art in their living room.

top Storage with a Gothic twist.

bottom The cool neutral tones of limestone set off the jade colour palette beautifully. Elegantly architectural candlesticks continue the Gothic theme.

A LOOK AT THE DETAILS

Hanging a long mirror between windows enhances natural daylight and was a decorative device much used in the 18th century. A traditionally carved Gothic mirror is one of the few truly antique elements in the scheme.

The jade wall colour was matched to the rich green damask so that the scheme had a unified, tailored feel. Using the same colour in a variety of textures creates a multi-layered effect without seeming cluttered.

The spiky shapes of Gothic architecture were reincarnated in oiled, fret-cut steel, but simplified for a more contemporary look. Arts and Crafts elements, such as the lamp bases, play a part in this Gothic revival.

The specially designed, repeated arch form, executed in oak, cropped up on the rood-screen above the fireplace and on the front of the sideboard doors. The honey-toned richness of the oak was an important colour accent in the predominantly green scheme.

The bespoke windows used a variety of handmade cathedral glasses to great effect. More brightly-coloured stained glass in these rather convoluted panels would have over-balanced what was an essentially restrained scheme.

A pale limestone floor and woven rug make a simple, almost monastic statement that rather cheekily subverts the rich finishes and fabrics used elsewhere in the room.

inside
GARDEN DESIGN
out

inside**out**
AN INTRODUCTION
TO GARDEN DESIGN

above This garden reflects the clients' request for a traditional, romantic style with an exciting focal point.

Until fairly recently, the choice of garden styles available to us has been very limited and often, especially for the suburban dweller, design was dictated almost solely by function. A pathway probably went straight down the garden, beneath the washing line, and the lawn took the form of a wall-to-wall carpet with a margin of borders. Self-expression was limited to crazy paving and a cocktail of herbaceous planting. Style and design were associated primarily with interiors, our clothes and our cars. Having a garden designed, or attempting to do it ourselves, seemed like a complicated, arcane business involving the mysteries of the soil, unpredictable plants and their dreadful Latin names.

Indoors, we know that our rooms need to work on a practical level, accommodating our furniture, our taste, and our living and entertainment needs. During the past few decades, we've felt more at home with making choices of colours and patterns, and become brave in creating schemes that make us feel comfortable in our environment. Well, the same applies in gardens. A garden should also be a place that we feel comfortable with – a place we love and one that works for every member of the household. Forget the mystery – by simply defining your requirements, you can develop a successful plan to create a place that suits you.

YOUR REQUIREMENTS
The most important decisions you will make when planning your garden are those that define what you want from it. The options are simple and logical: Are you an avid gardener; is the garden to be primarily

a place to grow plants in? Do you want a cooking or dining area? Somewhere to sunbathe or relax in? Somewhere to play? Somewhere to party? Considering all your requirements helps define your design.

Who is the garden for?

Your design may have to serve many different demands, which depend on how the garden will be used and by whom, as well as how much time will be spent there. Is it to be a family garden for children to play in, or do you crave a sophisticated, adult space for entertaining? Perhaps, like many of us, you need both?

If you want an adult space, you're probably considering a space for dining and entertaining in the evening, which will lead you to think about a hard surface or patio area. If the garden is to be a haven of tranquillity and peace, you'll need to consider how you might provide privacy – perhaps by creating an outdoor room?

above In West London we created an Islamic-influenced garden. This design was for a family from Pakistan who did not feel at home in a very English setting.

left The sharp green foliage of this tree fern looks beautiful against the cobalt blue surface of this outdoor, glass coffee table.

In a garden that has to cater for many needs, dividing it into separate 'rooms' has the potential to give everyone their own space. It's a great way of breaking up a plot, particularly the rectangular, suburban ones that many of us have, and, as well as being practical, it invariably adds interest and intrigue.

Children bring their own set of needs to a garden – an open space for games, pathways for bicycles, or tree houses and dens. All affect the choice of materials and structures throughout the garden, because obvious and subtle dangers abound in hard surfaces, buildings and even plants.

Access

Access is something we often have to take into account in *Home Front*, and it always affects the design, especially when our plans involve major excavation or building work. It is one of the most important factors in any garden plan and it's one you need to consider at the earliest stage. You'll need space to bring materials into your garden and room for more obvious things, such as pathways, to go through or around it.

If rear access to your garden is restricted, or impossible, all materials will have to be carried through your house – unless you're lucky enough to have a friendly neighbour who'll grant access through their plot. This can have a bearing on the design of the garden for long-term use too – you might decide against planting a high-maintenance garden if it means you have continually to transport bags of compost and garden debris through the house.

Within the garden, paths and similar hard land-scaping can dominate the visual appearance; so exploit this to your advantage by creating routes through the plot that combine practicality with style.

A low- or high-maintenance garden?

There's simply no point in laying out a garden crammed full of demanding plants if you don't have the time to look after them – you'll end up with an unsatisfactory, weedy wilderness rather than your desired structural planting. Decide how much time you will have to spend in the garden, and then decide how much of that time you want to spend tending it. Be honest with yourself about what you can manage. Your garden should be your dream plot – not a nightmare.

Sitting or dining area

A place for chairs and a table is always desirable, no matter how small the plot, and it should be one of the first areas you locate on your plan. You may prefer it in an area with maximum sunlight – either during the day, or in the evening to catch the last rays, but if you're not a sun-worshipper and like the idea of eating in a shady spot, you'll probably have more choice of where to position it. Some people prefer to put their dining area near to the house and kitchen, simply for convenience.

Seating doesn't have to be confined just to the patio though. Resting places around the garden will provide spaces to stop and enjoy a view or a particular plant, and will allow you to follow the sun around the garden without dragging the furniture with you. Seats can be

merely practical, but they may also provide a sculptural element in the garden, so choose carefully if they are to stay in position all year round. Concrete works really well in this respect, and can look beautiful. Forget its utilitarian image; it's a material I've used often in gardens as seating and as sculptural features. But if that's too modern for you, there is a huge range of attractive seating available in more traditional materials, such as wood, as well as in the ultra-contemporary materials like concrete and stainless steel.

Outdoor rooms

When it all gets too much and you need some privacy away from the noise and stress, the garden can be the perfect retreat. An outdoor room can provide a place for relaxation and peace, a place to work, or a den for children to play in or hide from siblings. The room doesn't need to be totally enclosed; sometimes partial enclosure can be enough just to make it feel sheltered from the rest of the garden and the activities that go on there. The Herne Hill garden (see page 13) included a metal structure that was designed to be used as a place to sit and contemplate; it provided a feeling of shelter and protection, but without the sense of claustrophobia that can result from total enclosure.

Privacy and noise

The desire for privacy in our gardens is almost universal, but bear in mind that there's a fine line between shutting out prying eyes and caging yourself in. Walls and fences are the most obvious solution when creating

a private space, but you'll need to check the building regulations because there are restrictions on boundaries over 2.2m (7ft) high.

Excavating to create a sunken plot is an excellent alternative for creating a garden room that is out of sight. This, however, may affect land drainage so, in this case, you may have to consider installing a sump pump to prevent your sunken patio from turning into a pond.

Screens can also be created around your plot simply by planting. Apart from the discredited Leyland cypress, possible choices include bamboos, silver birch and eucalyptus. They can provide year-round interest, but be aware that they may need occasional control. Bamboos make a wonderful rustling sound in the breeze and are the perfect choice if you want

to distract attention from unwanted noise around you.

The distraction principle is a clever way to mask unwanted sounds: by creating another, more attractive source of noise, you'll help divert attention from more troublesome sounds. Running water features or splashing fountains are excellent solutions if you don't want to use planting. They combine use with beauty too, in that they'll provide an attractive focal point.

Special requirements

As I have already said, children have their own special requirements in a garden space – safety is always paramount. But the same is also true for gardeners with special needs, especially for those with restricted mobility. In Shepherd's Bush, London, we created a

garden for Rudi, a wheelchair user, which needed careful planning to come up with an attractive, yet practical, design (see page 122). In this particular case, I didn't need to use raised beds because Rudi had help with the gardening, but I did have to plan for non-slip surfaces and uncluttered spaces so that he could move his chair around safely without causing damage to himself or the plants.

Generally speaking, though, raised beds are a fine idea for wheelchair-bound gardeners and are also a perfect solution for anyone who finds kneeling or bending a problem; the plants are raised to a level where they can be tended with ease.

Storage space

Paraphernalia goes hand-in-hand with gardening, DIY and children, so it's almost inevitable that some sort of

opposite Vibrant colour used on this pink outdoor room helps to create a happy atmosphere.

right A series of reclaimed brick arches beside a sunken paved area create a Gothic-style themeland.

far right At night, real magic is created by means of light and shadow.

outdoor storage space will be needed. There's no doubt that sheds and outhouses can be ugly so, if it's going to be visible, you need to think carefully about what style of building you want or can afford. If your budget will stretch to it, you can install an attractive structure that plays a part in the overall design. Otherwise, if you've inherited a monstrosity that you can't afford to replace, you'll find that dark green or black paint is very useful in toning down or disguising sheds or fences. Or, if you're clever, you can make them melt into the background by clothing them with climbing plants or wall shrubs.

Budget

Your budget is a major consideration in any scheme, and one that will inevitably affect your plans. It may be that some features from your wish list, such as natural stone flooring, may have to be sacrificed for a less expensive option, but there are lots of visually appealing substitutes on the market, so do your research thoroughly.

Often, the most carefully planned budget is exceeded; so don't beat yourself up over it if you have spent a little more than you intended. If money is really tight, however, phasing your plans can be the best way to achieve the garden you really want. If you plan your design carefully, you can develop the garden one section at a time and the overall scheme can be built up gradually, as and when you can afford it. Alternatively, you might be able simply to renovate your existing garden and even salvage some aspects of the design or planting.

YOUR DESIRES

Having worked your way through the requirements, let's enjoy the infinite possibilities of how your new garden will look. Dream and imagine your perfect plot. Really let your imagination go so that you get the feel for what you want; look for the essence of your beautiful new garden in your own mind's eye.

On *Home Front*, we ask clients to prepare a tearsheet presentation so that we can get an idea of their personal style and what they do and don't like. It's an excellent exercise – for both client and designer – because it really makes you work hard and consider all of the options.

Inspiration

Flicking through magazines and becoming a gardening programme junkie have their place, but it's a truism that the camera often lies. By becoming a garden tourist – snooping round your friends' plots, and visiting other gardens or garden shows – you'll be filled with ideas and true inspiration. It's like the difference between the theatre and the movies – an added intensity and excitement is experienced in the flesh.

Innovation can be good and, if that's what you want, be bold and have confidence in it. Everybody's different – you don't have to follow the neighbours. The garden should reflect your personal style and be somewhere that you feel comfortable and at home. In one garden, I designed a Gothic-inspired scheme for a couple who loved comics and Gothic style – it was a fantasy garden, but it was also a real garden that catered for all their practical needs.

far left Flamboyant lines and shapes combine to create a camp haven.

left Rolled mild steel bars develop an elegance when used in stepped formation.

Some styles and features that have appeared in interior schemes for a long time are now making the move out into the garden, as people become more adventurous. Ethnic influences have long featured in both interior and garden design in this country. With today's desire for low-maintenance plots and a serene place to retreat and relax, the minimalist Japanese style, for example, has become very popular. But as we head off on our holidays to exotic destinations, we are starting to bring back a taste of other, more diverse cultures and inspirations which we then incorporate into our designs.

Recently, I have had two opportunities to design gardens on an ethnic theme. One of these gardens used ornate trelliswork and deep, rich colours to enclose a sunken dining area that reflected the oriental background of its owners (see page 95). Another scheme gave me the opportunity to use hot, vibrant colours and planting to create a sense of modern Mexico (see pages 98 and 102).

The opportunity to design a garden using an ethnic theme is always fun, so don't be afraid to bring a touch of the exotic into your garden. If you feel a desert landscape looks out of place in the wet British weather, why not just incorporate elements of a particular style, then modernize or reinterpret them in your design to make them your own. Open your mind to all the influences around you, no matter how unconventional they may seem – incorporating whatever it is that inspires you most will guarantee that you create an original design.

GETTING DOWN TO THE DESIGN

Once you've established the mood and style of the garden that you want, go back to your list of practical considerations. This is the time that you may need to compromise and modify some elements of your dream design. For instance, you may need to abandon the idea of a large, deep pond until the children are older, but there's no reason why you shouldn't dig the hole now and get a few years' use out of it as a sandpit, until you can safely replace the sand with water.

Before you decide on where anything in the garden should go, take time to observe your plot carefully. Ideally, you should give yourself a year to see where the sun falls throughout the seasons and throughout each day, so that you'll know exactly where best to place a patio, or to site particular plants. Spending time now will be rewarded later, when your layout benefits from the sun at the best time of day to suit you, and your plants are all thriving in the best possible conditions.

So, take out a pen and paper and mark up all the features you know you must incorporate and where they should go – the patio, the shed, and any permanent features, such as drains, oil tanks or existing trees. Once you have done this, you can start thinking about the rest of the design. Many plots are square or rectangular, but that doesn't restrict you to designs with straight lines – a garden can be made to look deceptively large by incorporating circles or curves. If you're not a fan of strong geometry, hard lines can be softened by planting.

Focal points are important in your garden and the shape and flow of the lines of your plot can be used

right A sprig of *Laurus nobilis* (bay) displays its dark foliage against a vibrant yellow wall.

far right A curved, brick wall includes a circular opening to frame life beyond.

to direct the viewer's attention towards a particularly beautiful view or feature. They act as a trick to fool the eye, and can be a clever way of leading a visitor through one part of the garden and into another, while diverting their gaze away from unsightly objects.

Laying cables and pipes

If you are thinking of including any lighting or power points around the garden, or in outdoor rooms or dens, this is the time to plan where they should go. You don't want to lay down hard landscaping only to have to rip it up later to lay power cables, nor do you want them running across the surface of the garden where they'll be difficult to disguise. Water features usually require some sort of ducting – be it for water or electricity – so these should be laid and tested before covering the cables with hard surfaces.

Materials

Part of your design considerations will be your choice of materials. What you use in your garden will instantly set the scene for your design, but that doesn't mean you have to stick to just modern or traditional materials – a bit of both can work really well. A word of warning though – in this case, less is more. Don't try to include the whole range of materials or your plot will look as cluttered as a builders' merchant's yard and the effect of the design will be lost. Choose hard landscaping materials that you really like and that you think you'll enjoy for a long time; don't build concrete walls just

because they are trendy. They'll be a real challenge to remove when the fashion has passed and you can no longer stand the sight of them.

Think carefully about the materials you want to use – some may need specialist installation and this has implications for your budget. Consider, too, their suitability and durability for particular areas of your plot – decking, for example, is hugely popular, but it can be a hazard in damp and shady conditions if it becomes slippery with moss. Painted concrete and wooden fences will also require some maintenance, in that they will need re-painting or staining at some point in the future. Cobbles, gravel and metal grills are smart, durable materials that require little maintenance, but they are not very comfortable underfoot and so aren't ideal everywhere. Glass is a fabulous material that works really well in the garden, but even if you use toughened glass, you need to consider how safe it is for your project.

Colour

Let's face it; Britain isn't a country of bright sunshine all year round, so you'll probably want to introduce some

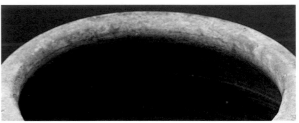

colour into your garden for those dull summer or winter days. Now, of course, there is a vast array of paints and wood stains on the market, so you need not suffer orange wooden fences any more. But don't go mad, keep the colours simple and the range to a minimum if you want them to be effective; don't try to paint everything in sight in all the colours of the rainbow. A few, carefully selected statement shades work best and give just enough colour to brighten the space.

Colour can also be used as an accent throughout the garden, to link the spaces; blue, aubergine and pink look wonderful in all kinds of light. Darker shades can be used to disguise unsightly objects. Shades of deep green and black are perfect choices for toning down structures and helping them disappear; brown is equally effective, but don't use it in any other way because it's almost a non-colour in a garden context and doesn't give enough contrast.

Planting

Plants are an essential part of a garden, even in a minimalist scheme. Design your planting plan to suit the style of your garden. If you have gone for a minimalist scheme, for instance, you will probably want a few spectacular, architectural plants rather than borders crammed full of flowers and shrubs. Plants are a fantastic way of introducing form and colour to a garden. Strong architectural outlines can echo strong, designed forms and lines, and lend height and substance to beds and borders. Herbaceous plants, shrubs and climbers can be used equally well to soften strong lines and hard surfaces.

Think about the effect you want to achieve, the time you have to care for the plants, the aspect of your garden and, very importantly, the type of soil you have. Don't be put off by this list – it's much simpler than you think. Once you've done this little bit of research, head down to your garden centre armed with clear ideas. Garden centres and nurseries can overwhelm you with choice, but, if you go with a list of ideal plants, you'll come away with something you want, rather than buying a load of highly unsuitable plants that have been placed temptingly within your reach. If you want plants to thrive, choose the ones that you know are appropriate for your site and situation.

opposite Rendered concrete walls which frame the views in a small garden are adorned in two shades of hot pink.

right Close up, the reinforcing bar looks like a tangled mess, but, as you can see from the shadow it casts, the greater picture is a beautiful, spherical nest.

When deciding on your planting plan, think about whether you prefer mostly foliage or flowers – remember that foliage always lasts longer than flowers. Decide whether you want a range of colours and shapes all year round, or whether you actually enjoy the evidence of changing seasons. Evergreen plants provide shape and colour throughout the year and help prevent the garden looking sad in the winter months; deciduous plants, such as dogwood, silver birch and twisted hazel, have fabulous stems that look wonderful when leafless. Think about flowering plants, such as winter-flowering jasmine, hellebores and snowdrops, which bring colour at winter's end heralding the riot of colour from spring-flowering bulbs and shrubs. And, of course, the summer brings forth a huge choice of colour in permanent plantings, which can be supplemented by annuals and biennials.

If you like the idea of colour and you are prepared to sit down and plan your scheme carefully, go for a colour-themed garden. You can use tones, hues and shades of one or two colours to create unity, but remember that too many varied colours can sometimes work against you and even in the most riotously coloured borders, less is usually more. If an array of colour in your beds is not really your thing, you can make as simple a statement as the White Garden at Sissinghurst. Beware of monotone themes though; they can be truly monotonous without at least a modicum of emphatic colour contrast.

THE CASE STUDIES

On *Home Front*, Laurence and I are lucky enough to be invited into people's homes and gardens and asked to create their dream visions. It's always a collaboration getting to grips with what somebody really wants. In the garden, I feel an obligation always to have something new to say. The ability to create different spaces for a whole range of people, to excite people about the art of design and the craft of gardening is great fun. And because every person is different, every garden will also be unique. As you'll see from the case studies, our gardens are not to everyone's taste. But what I hope they do is to make people consider the possibilities of what a garden can be.

out HOLLYWOOD CHIC

above Stepped lawns, art mosaic pools, gleaming terrazzo and a revolving glitterball egg combine to create a flamboyant style.

opposite The egg opens like an over-size Fabergé creation, to reveal a cabinet full of its rocket fuel.

THE DESIGN

Inspiration can come from many sources, but it's sometimes hard to find. This house was a grand statement of a very distinctive architectural period – so how could this translate to the garden? Exterior style on an Art Deco theme is difficult to pinpoint.

What evolved – after many sketches – was a design quite different to the one I had first imagined. I expected strong straight lines and brutal white walls: modernism that was theatrical yet solid. Yet what arrived was pure 1930s Hollywood – Busby Berkeley movie sets, Hall of Fame stars and sheer decadence. Mixed with props from a rock concert, this garden had decided it was going to be something else. And that was glamorous!

The patio became a raised terrace that flowed from the back door in waves. The main lawn was flanked on either side by smaller lawns that stepped in unison. Two deep-blue, mosaic pools, with six dancing fountains in brass, were reminiscent of bathing beauties in synchronous unity. At the far end a huge, glitterball egg revolved as if to show its best side, in its belly a cocktail cabinet whose contents could only enhance the enjoyment of this surreal design.

The whole scheme evolved from a need for high drama, not least because this was a garden that was to be appreciated from a great height. The primary viewing points were from the roof terrace and the terrazzo.

Shape, form and line

Different lines introduced into a plot can create great excitement. Simple, basic shapes with strong lines and

The Clients

Simon and Heather and their four children had always been quite content living in the area, but there was a house locally that had held a fascination for Simon since he was pushed past it in his pram. It was called Blue Rails and it was an Art Deco house of great architectural significance, with wonderful style and flair. And now they lived there, and their mission was to restore it to its former glory and add some magic in the garden. This was a project with real passion.

The Plot

If there is such a thing as a happy suburban plot, this was it. The atmosphere felt good, it felt right. The garden was fine, even pretty, but posed a problem. How did it fit with the house? Shrub borders hugged the perimeter around huge swathes of lawn; a few concrete slabs, surrounded by balustrade walling and a washing line, posed as a patio. It was suburban and lacked panache. It was an undistinguished afterthought.

The Brief

The family wanted a garden that reflected and suited the period of the house. But they were at a loss to know what this meant. Our thoughts turned to something modern and linear. An essence of televised adaptations of Agatha Christie's Poirot came to mind. They liked architectural planting, uncluttered lines and strong structure. A sense of order, peace and control were the desired effect. Dislikes included anything 'frilly' and the wild, overgrown look. An area for their children to enjoy and play in was essential.

curves can be the best foundation for a design. Lines and curves offer endless permutations, but over-use makes your plot feel fussy and cluttered – so keep it simple. Form was embodied here in both hard structures and planting, but you could use planting to soften strong lines for less definition.

At Blue Rails, these dramatic forms echoed the Art Deco style, which was reinforced by giving each part of the garden its mirror image. I created this by finding the central line and using the same template on both sides of it. Marking out is a huge part of turning plans into reality, so don't rush it – it's best to expend energy on getting shapes right first time, rather than struggling to correct them later. Here, the roof terrace made a great vantage point from which to supervise marking out.

Flooring

Different materials create different feelings, so consider the essence of what you are trying to achieve. In an over-the-top garden like this, we needed a unique flooring that expressed luxury and glamour; something that would literally sparkle. And vivid pink terrazzo proved perfect.

Rediscovering such a glamorous old material brings a sense of delight, but also a responsibility to consider whether it would be suitable, durable and achievable. Only then could we enjoy it and exploit its potential to the fullest effect.

Terrazzo is the polished surface that was used in the Hollywood Hall of Fame. Made from marble chips in a cement matrix and laid on a bed of scree, it is an

left The egg in winter!

opposite right The pool and stepped lawns clad in brass strips were reminiscent of the Busby Berkeley movie sets.

opposite left To fulfill the requirements of all the family, a climbing frame and rocking boat were installed for the children.

undeniably expensive surface that needs a professional to lay it properly. If you don't want the hassle, you can buy terrazzo tiles with a similarly wonderful, shiny, marble finish. Here, the pink terrazzo swept in waves down to the lawn, and we used inlaid brass strips to break up the solid colour.

Focal points

Focal points are created by directing the eye to one spot by means of planting, or by the line of forms or structures within the garden. Often, a single, centrally placed feature grabs attention immediately – and this garden cried out for this approach. I was aiming for maximum drama, so my focal point had to make a major statement when seen from the house. The lawn was laid out in a shape that seemed to lead up to something – elegance, a flourish.

First ideas, which proved too costly or too dangerous, included a bronze statue of a woman rising slowly from a sunken shaft. This might have lent more of an air of understated elegance and panache, but camp won out, and so the disco version of the Fabergé egg was born. My egg was inspired by a Spinal Tap moment when the rock group U2 had arrived on stage during the Pop tour in a giant lemon with a surface like a mirror ball!

But I wanted something that would revolve, I wanted some movement, I wanted a jewel. Because the form is fairly basic, an egg that glittered seemed achievable. It was glamorous, if a little silly, but more practically, it contained essences central to the Art Deco period – cocktails. Adults could enjoy it, children would love it,

it would show off. Our egg was laid in a Basildon factory and caused much mirth on its journey to Luton on the back of a truck. Sunday worshippers stopped, gawped and pointed. It smiled back at them. And once in place it sparkled.

An area for children

As in most family gardens, it was important to create some adult space, but it was also essential to create an area in which the children could play safely – without sacrificing the glamour and sophistication of the design.

The pools of water around the lawn were only 30cm (1ft) deep. The parents were clearly aware of the responsibility of water in a garden where there are children. Of course, it is not just the children who live in the house, but child visitors to the garden that are at risk. These pools were designed so that they could be drained and used as sunken areas if necessary.

To one side of the design – well away from the egg, the focal point of the plot – we covered an area with play bark and erected a wooden climbing frame. By locating the play area away from the carefully designed, central section of the garden, and by using natural materials to blend the structures into the background, this space provided a practical playground that was within sight of adults, but which did not detract from the design.

Planting

As this design was based on very strong forms and lines, I wanted the planting to enhance rather than lessen the effect. Highly stylized planting created structure and definition. The planting scheme was predominantly evergreen so as to lessen the impact of winter. Italian cypress (*Cupressus sempervirens*), phormiums and a low-growing cherry laurel (*Prunus laurocerasus* 'Otto Luyken'), flanked the entrance to the garden in curving beds that mirrored each other.

Elegantly curved borders swept around the lawns and pools, framed by a low, formal hedge of box (*Buxus sempervirens).* A second, outer ring was planted, using evergreen *Fatsia japonica* to add height. At the end of the garden, as a background to the egg, a small grove of silver birch trees (*Betula pendula*) would provide winter interest with their beautiful bark.

A LOOK AT THE DETAILS

 Lights scattered all around the water's edge lent night-time highlights – for aesthetic and safety reasons. Lighting the egg drew the eye strongly to the focal point by night, and its scattered reflections provided extra illumination.

 Phormiums are a wonderful 'architectural' plant that provide bold structure and form. Very dark-leaved varieties like *Phormium tenax* Purpureum Group add sophistication and dark year-round colour, offset by the green lawn. Other forms are available with colour flashes on the leaves, in shades of orange, pink or white.

 The egg gave a real sense of drama to the scheme. Encased in mirror tiles, it reflected the surrounding planting by day and the lights beneath it at night. Of course, it had a practical function too, with a fridge inside for glamorous evening entertaining.

 Birch trees add height and draw the eye down from the tree tops to the egg below. The white bark brings light and colour into the garden throughout the year, especially when reflected in the mirror tiles of the rotating egg.

 Strong lines are softened by planting and the hard surface is defined by the contrasting lawn that surrounds it. Planting was kept to a minimum and at a fairly low level, so as not to detract from the design's structure.

 These sunken troughs were lined with cobalt blue tiles to bring a touch of rich colour to the garden. The pools could be simple, still-water features, or wonderful leaping fountains could be switched on for added drama.

out PAVILION IN THE SKY

above A slice of aeroplane wing creates a roof for this glass pavilion, while a simple bed of architectural-style planting is surrounded by a shallow moat of reflective water.

opposite New retaining walls have been clad in simple sheets of stainless steel. Aluminium steps lead from one level to another.

THE DESIGN

Short, wide plots are a common dilemma and can be awkward to manage. If the longest axis of a garden is parallel to, rather than at right angles to the house, the eye is drawn to the boundary, which emphasizes its lack of depth. In such a plot, you need to trick the eye, drawing it into the garden by creating a space that invites exploration. This can be done in a number of ways, from dramatic planting to using pieces of sculpture as focal points. Water is also a powerful way to maintain focus within the garden.

In this case, the basis of the new design was to appreciate the changing levels and use contemporary materials to create interest. The design evolved from an unusual perspective. Living between London and Dublin, I am a regular commuter by aeroplane and I have always had a child-like fascination with flying. Gazing through the porthole window on to the sleek metallic wings has long intrigued me, and watching planes approach Heathrow Airport in a row

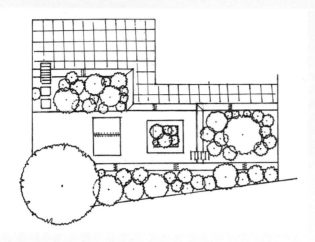

The Clients

John and Kate were moving into an early semi-retirement. They were starting to spend time, money and energy on refurbishing their dream home – a beautiful period house. John was a real handyman, while Kate was a gardener. What they wanted from the garden was something unique, as well as something special, practical, beautiful and in keeping with their style. A look at their home revealed an appreciation of tradition, but with a desire to add a contemporary edge.

The Plot

The garden was an awkward shape, running along the width of the house, but it did benefit from a mature horse chestnut, established shrubs and old walls, and interesting features with potential for adaptation, such as different ground levels and an old concrete pond.

The Brief

John and Kate were very clear from the start about what they wanted. Kate was fairly definite about the style of the garden, while John's domain was the house. They were agreed on the basic requirements. Water was a must in the design, but not in the form of a conventional pond. Garden lighting was also required. They wanted the planting to continue the old and new' theme, choosing some New World plants as well as European herbaceous favourites. A lawn was definitely an option, but not an absolute necessity, and the garden should contain a place to sit and relax, both sheltered and open.

with just a couple of minutes' distance between them, is just mad. Design inspiration has often come from modes of transport – cruise liners and trains added enormously to the sense of freedom and achievement that featured in the Art Deco style. Seeing these sleek birds cross a clear autumnal evening sky – linked with John's association with a helicopter company – got me thinking.

The garden retained its different levels but new walls were clad in curved stainless steel. A pavilion, which was in effect a glass box, was given an aerofoil-shaped steel roof. The paving materials were white, the steps to different levels were aluminium, but otherwise, shapes were kept simple. Lights were sunk into the lawn almost like runway lights. A square, aluminium water rill became the border for an island bed of architectural planting.

Connecting inside and out

Despite the period nature of the house, John and Kate had decided on a very modern extension featuring large expanses of glass. This made the connection with my

above A shallow, square rill encloses an island of planting – edged by lawn on the other side, it retains a clean, elegant feel.

top right The amazing purple berries of *Callicarpa bodinieri* var. *giraldii* 'Profusion' contain such vivid colour that they appear unreal.

modern garden very easy. And the sleekness of Laurence's interior materials, such as the dark floor tiles, contrasted beautifully with my natural stone paving.

Of course, you could make the connection between house and garden using plants. Climbers are very effective in merging inside and out as they clothe and soften the architecture. Or, when considering hard materials for the garden – concrete, brick or even railway sleepers – think about how they might contrast with or complement the framework of the house, according to your preferences.

In this garden, the area for the ground-floor patio was widened, to aid access from the garden room and to give space to view the raised garden from a slight distance.

What to keep

Before you charge in and bulldoze everything in sight, take a good look around – there may be something worth keeping. Established plants provide valuable structure and a sense of maturity in a newly-designed plot. Be cautious about felling mature trees – you may repent their loss later and they might even have preservation orders on them, a point worth investigating. In John and Kate's garden there was much to conserve – a beautiful mature horse chestnut, some well-established shrubs, lovely old walls and dozens of specimens that Kate had rescued from her last garden.

When designing your garden it's always best to work with your site and make the most of what's there. In this case, we modified slightly the different levels

right The glass pavilion, set under the shade of an existing horse chestnut tree, is the perfect place to recline in the garden while reading the Sunday papers.

that already existed in the garden, but the old pond was completely excavated to be replaced by a new and contemporary water feature that was much more in keeping with this modern garden.

Using different levels

Raised beds are a great way to create different levels. They bring plants nearer to eye level and can make you feel that you're surrounded by vegetation. They also create opportunities to introduce interesting hard materials into the garden, either natural ones, like reclaimed railway sleepers, or more contemporary ones.

Even traditional gardens can be given a subtle twist by introducing modern materials. Don't be afraid to experiment with steel, aluminium or glass, but do choose only materials that you really like and appreciate. When using modern materials, also bear in mind that some will require expert installation and may have special maintenance requirements.

Here we clad the retaining walls of the beds in satin-finished stainless steel. After much experimentation we arrived at a shape reminiscent of the structure of an aeroplane wing.

Adapting a construction technique used for aircraft wings in the past, we built fins from marine ply with a supporting cage of narrow timbers. These were mounted on the bed walls and covered with satin-finish, stainless sheet steel that was rivetted into place. The metal gave a cool, modern feel to the garden, but didn't overpower the design and was softened by lush planting.

Outdoor room

Many of us fantasize about creating a haven in which to escape the world and there's no better location for it than an outdoor room in the garden. It's a place in which you can enjoy the garden, perhaps taking shade from sun or shelter from rain. It will form a strong focal point, so it needs to be in keeping with the feel of your garden. A traditional summer house would be out of place here. We wanted a structure in keeping with the aerodynamic theme of the garden, so the glass pavilion with its metal grill floor and mirror-finished steel columns beneath the radical, stainless steel aerofoil roof was perfect.

A LOOK AT THE DETAILS

The pavilion made a strong focal point, and its metal grill floor, mirror-finished columns and stainless steel roof linked up with Laurence's room, which projected into the garden. It also provided a practical, all-weather place from which to admire the garden from a different angle.

Creating different levels instantly provides interest. Raised beds break up a difficult shape and create focal points to deflect the view from the boundaries. The planted levels also give the plot height, which draws the eye up into the garden.

Stainless steel edging adds a contemporary touch to a traditional style of planting. The shiny metal sets off and reflects foliage and strongly defines the shape of the garden, while providing a sense of continuity by visually linking the various levels and beds.

A central raised bed, with a water rill surrounding dramatic planting, maintains focus within the garden. Made from aluminium, it echoed the use of metal elsewhere in the garden and its reflective properties shone out perfectly in combination with water.

The tree fern, *Dicksonia antarctica* and phormiums are spectacular plants. Such striking foliage makes a strong statement in its own right as well as softening the lines of a highly structured design. Architectural plants can also accentuate existing planting, as they did here, highlighting the mature trees, a horse chestnut and a liquidambar.

Spot and spike lights were strategically placed around the garden. Spike lights uplit trees for drama, while sunken spots marked out the central bed and water feature, the light reflecting off the metal beds on two sides. In the pavilion, halogen lights were suspended beneath the metal grill floor to create a dramatic, sculptural feel.

out RURAL RETREAT

above Two rusting spheres, sited on top of a circular paved area and leaning against one, act as transparent sculptural forms.

THE DESIGN

A sloping garden brings one surprising benefit – that of immediate built-in interest. It may not seem immensely practical but, if planned properly, a slope excites the natural instinct of curiosity, either inducing the eye to wander, or inspiring the sense of adventure that leads you to embark on a full exploration.

Terracing is a very effective way of dealing with awkward inclines. By simply levelling, or cutting out flat areas into the side of the slope, terracing creates functional and attractive spaces. The gentle incline of this yard was broken up into three large, circular cobbled surfaces that were level, but linked by gently sloping pathways. A gravity-assisted water rill, with a recirculating pump, flowed around the site and a bridge over the rill linked the paved areas to make access for the children's bikes and scooters easier. The lower patio near the kitchen became an area for outdoor dining and entertaining, with views into the garden in one direction, and to the vista beyond in the other.

Focal points

Often, when laying out gardens, the major design concern is to keep attention within the garden so as to deflect the eye from ugly exterior features or neighbouring houses. If, however, you enjoy the benefit of a view – perhaps a city landmark from a roof garden, or one of the surrounding countryside, it would be a shame not to incorporate it into your design.

So observe your view well. See how you can make the most of it either by leaving it open or by framing it with

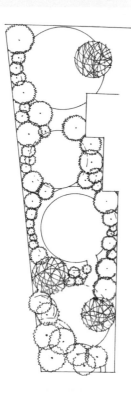

The Clients

Malcolm and Sarah, with their two small children, had fulfilled their dream of moving from busy London life to a small rural village. They were settling into country life on the edge of picturesque Shotteswell.

The Plot

The site of the garden was an old concrete milkyard at the back of the house. It was a long time since the property had been used as a farm, and the yard was now a glorified rubbish tip. Its narrow, rectangular shape sloped down gently and enjoyed beautiful views over the Warwickshire countryside. Full sun only existed in a small area beside the kitchen.

The Brief

The requirements from this uninviting site were a place for relaxation, entertainment and somewhere for the children to play. Since visitors entered the house through this back garden, the design needed to provide a high-impact solution.

Their personal style favoured a mix of traditional and modern with a planting plan which included lots of foliage in a naturalistic style that would blend in with the surrounding countryside.

top Azalea and heather combine to create winter and spring interest.

bottom Curved raised beds in the same local stone as the existing walls made new planting spaces.

plants or structures. Consider the possibilities of tantalizing glimpses from various parts of the garden – one enterprising designer in Paris installed a moveable hedge which operated automatically so that it was raised or lowered at the flick of a switch, therefore granting him privacy or openness.

But, most importantly, don't try to compete with a fine view; don't create artificial focal points where one exists naturally. In a rural setting the key can be an uncomplicated design.

Materials

A good appreciation of materials is essential. Your choice should be something that inherently feels right. In rural areas in particular, your garden should blend in effortlessly and not jar with the wider landscape. One way to achieve this is to use local materials, such as stone, for paving or walling, but it can be an expensive option.

The farmhouse was made of Hornton stone – a warm-coloured sedimentary stone. Supplies were obtained from a nearby quarry to construct our features, which were mainly raised beds.

It's important to be aware of the limited resources of planet Earth and to use them responsibly. We shouldn't have the right to use whatever material we want to create our havens. So consider your choice of materials carefully – salvaged materials can be an excellent option. Most of all, make sure anything you're using comes from a sustainable and environmentally responsible source.

Sculpture

It can be great fun to incorporate sculpture in to your garden. I love displaying objects outside because the look of them changes constantly; a gallery environment can be quite sterile, whereas outside, strong form can interact with light and shade, planting and water. In this way, magic can be created.

For this site, I wanted to introduce something that you could see through – sculptures of large scale that weren't over-dominant. Three spheres of varying diameters made from steel reinforcing bars were commissioned and sited for differing effects. They were inspired by a public Amnesty International sculpture of welded chains, in the form of a sphere that enclosed an eternal flame. They also had echoes of Anthony Gormley's twisted metal sculpture beside the Thames.

The idea behind these sculptures was to give perspective and add another dimension to our plot.

One sphere met you as you entered the garden; a second, much larger one was big enough for the children to get inside and use as a den. Then, as you worked your way down the paved garden, there was a final smaller one which could be rolled around.

These spheres were enjoyable just for their lovely shape, but, although they acted primarily as sculptural pieces, they also served as a contemporary arbour for climbing plants. Planted with honeysuckle, and allowed to rust to a striking burnt orange, they could only improve with time. We could have lacquered or powder-coated them to prevent rusting, but a certain magic is inherent in the idea that, if left, they would revert to soil.

Planting

Creating a planting plan is an incredibly personal task. You probably already have a list of favourite plants that you've used in a previous garden or seen elsewhere. Use these as the basis of your plan, but don't be afraid to use new varieties and don't shy away from plant trends either. Of course, the most important thing to consider when choosing plants is their suitability to their new home – their size, and their soil and aspect requirements. Some plants may survive in a less than ideal situation, but if you want them to flourish, it is better to follow the rules.

Sarah and Malcolm wanted an interesting, lush green garden that would provide colour right through the year. The garden was in shade for most of the day, so we needed to choose plants that required, or were at least

left A concrete rill of water snakes around the circular paving and is traversed by a cobbled bridge.

tolerant of shade. It's a common fallacy that colour is hard to find in a shady garden; there are many woodland plants, such as primulas and dicentras, that will provide a burst of colour. *Geranium* 'Johnson's Blue' copes with dappled shade and will reliably produce tonnes of fabulous blue flowers throughout the summer. If you are looking for ground cover, variegated plants such as *Euonymus* 'Silver Queen' will brighten up any dull corner.

Here the soil was acidic so we chose plants that require a lime-free soil. These include rhododendrons and azaleas, many of which grow naturally beneath a canopy of branches, and are available in just about any colour of the rainbow. Camellias, heathers and pieris are other good choices for this situation.

A mixture of trees, including *Betula* (birches), *Sorbus* (rowans) and a *Malus* 'John Downie' (crab apple tree), were planted along the roadside perimeter of the garden for privacy. A *Robinia pseudoacacia* (false acacia), with amazing lime-green foliage, was used to screen out the view of the house next door. The acid-loving conifer *Cryptomeria japonica* (Japanese cedar), which had been sculpted into a globe shape, took its place in a sheltered corner and echoed the circles and spheres in the garden. The lower patio, in the sunniest part of the garden, was encircled with a wide variety of aromatic and culinary herbs that added wonderful scents to the sitting area – including hyssop, parsley, thyme, lavender and sage.

A LOOK AT THE DETAILS

 Wire spheres provide focal points throughout the garden. Although made in a heavy industrial material, the overall effect is surprisingly delicate. When colonized by climbing plants, they will form organic green globes.

 This plant is perfectly suited to this acidic soil but can also happily withstand lime. *Erica* 'Kramer's Red' has dark, bronze-green foliage with deep purple-red flowers that provide rich winter colour.

 Clay cobbles arranged in a circular pattern add to the theme of circles and spheres and blend well with the stone of the house and garden walls, especially as I added a few paler-coloured cobbles to the pattern to create a more mottled effect. They are inexpensive and easy to use.

 Make the most of a view like this. Descending patios lead the eye down the garden towards the view, guided by the trees and sculptures positioned to either side.

 Water flows around the garden through concrete rills, and is recirculated via a pump and an underground tank. The water provides movement and added interest in the garden.

 The warmth of the Hornton stone sits beautifully in the wider landscape. This was the sunniest area of the garden, an ideal location for sun-loving culinary and aromatic herbs.

out PURE PATIO

above The wide expanse of decking completes the sculptural hideaway and the exotic planting makes this the perfect outdoor bachelor pad.

opposite Three fountains dance through a galvanized grill, but disappear at the the flick of a switch.

THE DESIGN

Small back gardens are very common in city and suburban areas and it can often be difficult to make them interesting; trying to fit too much into a restricted place is simply a lesson in clutter. The standard problems faced by inner-city dwellers are space, privacy and noise. So careful planning, as ever, is key.

Generally, no perfect solution exists, but an uninspiring plot *can* be successfully altered to create a personal haven. Acknowledging the limitations of the surroundings and compromising with the realities can lead to harmony. Sometimes, the answers can be quite simple. If you consider what you really want from a space, the lessons in how to achieve it will slowly emerge. Begin by asking yourself what you really want the garden for? Is it an open space, an entertaining space, or a space to be packed with plants? Will you be able to maintain it? Does your budget stretch to fulfil your desires?

For Rudi, outdoor flooring was very important. In this location, decking was the perfect solution. The aspect of the garden was open and sunny, so the danger of damp, slippery surfaces would not be an issue. Rather than construct complicated beds, I decided to confine most of the planting to the boundaries.

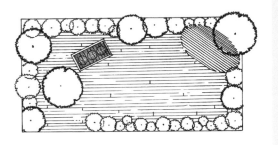

The Plot

Rectangular in shape, the garden consisted of a dull patio, a lawn area and boring borders. The 'relaxed' nature of the lawn meant that Rudi in his chair was confined to the small strip of slabs. Along with these restrictions, the garden was small and enclosed by high walls, but despite the walls was overlooked, creating the overwhelming feeling of constantly being watched rather than of peace or tranquillity.

The Brief

In this case what was needed was very clear: access and freedom to manoeuvre, which most of us take for granted. Rudi also wanted interesting plants, but not ones that required an awful lot of attention; materials that he had come across at different stages in his life, the sound of water to be central to his patio courtyard and a bold structure to create privacy, but not shelter. The garden also needed to be a picture from the living room and bedroom in Rudi's flat – it needed to be a pleasure to look at.

The Client

As a result of a skiing accident in his early years, Rudi was confined to a wheelchair and lived in a ground-floor flat in the heart of busy Shepherd's Bush in London. An energetic man, with a strong involvement in sports, Rudi liked modern uncluttered spaces and, having sampled the Californian lifestyle, he was a great fan of wooden decks. A lover of outdoor lifestyles, he was keen to have a garden that would be an outdoor room for him.

Rudi loved uncluttered spaces for aesthetic reasons, but here they served practically too, in that they allowed him free movement in his wheelchair.

For people of restricted mobility, raised beds can be an ideal solution, because planting and maintenance is undertaken at, or just above, waist level, without bending. As Rudi's use of his hands was extremely limited, raised beds were not a priority; a friend would help out with the limited gardening chores required.

A specimen tree was planted on an island within the deck to create interest. It also provided some dappled shade and framed the views from the living room. Water erupted at the press of a button from a mosaic pool beneath a metal grill set at the same level as the decking. The wheelchair could glide over the exposed grill when the water was turned off.

Privacy was a major requirement, so a secluded area was built in. Another factor in urban plots is noise pollution. Some people actually find the noise of passing traffic soothing, but most of us don't. The most successful remedy in this situation is to direct attention away from the offending source to a more pleasant one. The murmur

of water really helps in this respect, or you could use multipurpose bamboos; they act as a screen for privacy and help exclude noise, while providing their own relaxing sound as they rustle gently in the breeze.

An inner city patio may be a limited space but it can still achieve the essence of your idea of a garden.

dramatic shell – a cross between a cave and a gazebo, but ultimately inspired by an armadillo.

Circular or elliptical shapes are good lines to use in garden design, because they fit comfortably into most situations. In this small, rectangular garden, our armadillo, which had been created beautifully by a metal-work specialist, was lowered by crane into its appointed corner. An idea is one thing, but seeing its manifestation – especially dropping from a great height – is something else. When we saw it in place, we knew that it was meant to be. The relaxed lines worked well with the leafy planting. In a barren space, surrounded only by decking and brick walls, it might have looked brutal.

Garden buildings

Structures in gardens, such as arbours, pergolas and summerhouses, can serve many different purposes: privacy, shelter (from sun and rain), as adventurous focal points, or simply to support climbing plants. Drama and fun can be achieved, or subtlety and serenity. The way you use them is a personal choice. Don't automatically dismiss them as being too large and dominating before considering the opportunities that such a statement feature presents in creating a telling garden composition.

In this garden, I wanted to create something that would make a private haven, but which would also look good when viewed from the house. I decided on a simple sculptural shape that would also be useful. Straps of mild steel were curved into an ellipse to form a

Seating and sculpture

No patio would be complete without some sort of seating, whether it's for dining, sunbathing, or simply sitting down to enjoy the view. Choose your seating to suit your needs; there's a huge range of garden furniture available, and if comfort is your priority, go out and test your chairs before buying.

In this garden, I wanted to reflect the modern, sculptural feel of the armadillo arbour and decided on modern, concrete seating. These seats look fantastic and surprisingly, given the material, comfort did not suffer at all.

right A *Butia capitata*, or Jelly palm, acts as a specimen in the deck and frames the garden features.

Planting

Along with architectural structures, Rudi liked the strong, architectural plants that are now in vogue. These are plants that make statements with strong outlines or sculptural forms, as in the giant leaves of *Gunnera manicata*, or the aggressive spikes of a yucca. They add scale and substance to a garden, and even just one or two will create instant impact.

Plants such as palms and tree ferns provide real drama and a jungle feel, but, in our zeal to find something different, we sometimes forget that not all of them are hardy and may need some special winter care, or even moving indoors during the coldest months. In this sheltered garden, we used the magnificent Jelly palm, *Butia capitata*, as the main focal tree. Other appropriate, Planet Zog-type plants included *Arum pictum*, with darkly sinister flowers and large, arrow-shaped leaves; the banana plant, *Musa basjoo*, and the Rice-paper plant, *Tetrapanax papyrifer;* these last two have large leaves that die down in winter.

Combining evergreens and herbaceous plants produces a garden with colour and structure that looks good all year round, but which also changes with the seasons.

Lighting

The garden at night can become a theatre in which you choose the parts to highlight and the plants to be brought to centre stage. It's a time when you can cheat a little; it's you, not the sun, that gets to select what will be revealed.

Clever positioning of lights can serve a multitude of purposes: to uplight favourite or special plants, to create moods, to enhance seating areas or focal points, or, of course, to highlight pathways for safety's sake. Modern technology, from simple spot or solar lights, to neon or fibre-optic lighting, can be harnessed to provide exciting and dramatic effects.

At the more elemental end of the scale, fire always fascinates, and garden candles, lanterns and torch flames can add fairytale enchantment to the smallest of plots, without the need for fitting electrical cables.

Introducing lights to this garden ensured special night-time effects. A spotlight illuminated the large palm tree, whose geometric foliage cast intriguing patterns on the deck, and the metal armadillo was backlit to emphasize its structure and lend an element of mystery. Finally, a torch flame was added to the patio space by the house to bring a sense of fun and magic into this tropical garden.

A LOOK AT THE DETAILS

Screen planting around the edges of the garden gives the illusion that the garden is part of a larger whole, a clearing in a jungle forest perhaps. On a more practical level, the height and density of this planting provides shade and extra privacy, without blocking out all the light from the garden.

The armadillo arbour was specially made for the garden. Made of steel, it is a structure which is both brutal and beautiful. A perfect retreat for shade and privacy, it could be softened by planting climbers to scramble through it.

Grill water fountains give guests a surprise. This water feature takes up little space and presents no problems for a wheelchair. It is extremely safe because all the water is contained in a shallow reservoir beneath the grill. It looks great in the evening with lights playing on the fountain.

The cast-concrete seat is almost a work of art in itself. It's fantastic to look at, but it also makes a great garden seat with its durable construction and relatively light weight. Again, it is made from a brutal material because brutal was the theme of both the interior and exterior design.

Butia capitata is a dramatic evergreen palm that comes from Argentina. The grey-blue stems and strongly arching shape create a superb specimen tree. It is somewhat tender, but in sheltered areas it should be fine. As it is very slow growing I chose a large specimen to give instant impact.

Grooved decking gave an outdoor, Californian feel and the wooden flooring expanse was broken up and softened by the lush planting of palms, ferns and grasses. It's an easy surface to navigate by wheelchair and the deep grooving on the deck's surface also makes the patio safe, even after rain.

out
THE OUTDOOR LOUNGE

above Glass, stone and wood combine to create a feeling of unrestrained elegance.

opposite A concrete slab has been cut out of the roof of an underground bomb shelter, which, with the addition of a glass hat has turned into an elegant outside room.

THE DESIGN

The clients desired a Mediterranean feel and terracing the garden with three substantial levels worked both aesthetically and as a practical solution.

The first level was a deck stretching from the house. This led to a retaining wall and the reconstructed bomb shelter. For the next level, I designed an open room without a roof and with a floor of decking and plate-glass walls. Planting filled the straight beds on either side. The final terrace was a simple lawn, providing a soft playing area for the children and a green carpet that softened the highly defined lines of all the other materials.

Throughout the garden, retaining walls were constructed from gabions – wire baskets filled with white stone. These walls once again reflected the desire for natural materials and worked really well with the white, concrete-rendered walls. To create a sense of movement and excitement, and to link each terrace level visually, I designed a child-safe water rill – a series of silvered trays jutted out from the gabion walls, with re-circulating water cascading into concealed reservoirs.

White was the predominant colour of the materials, and this, set against the cooling green of the lawn and the sleekness of the glass, made a very stylish statement.

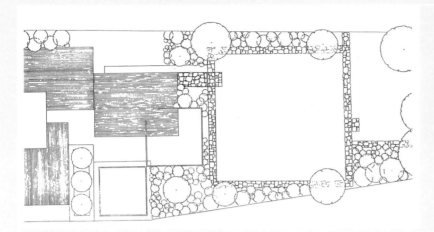

The Plot

The garden was big – 12m by 35m (38 ft by 80 ft) – and sloped down towards the house. It dropped dramatically by 1.5m (5 ft) as it neared the patio doors. But the seemingly unsurmountable problem was a completely intact air-raid shelter built from reinforced concrete.

The Clients

David and Amanda and their three children lived in a 1930s semi-detached house. They loved natural materials, such as stone, shells and wood, and wanted a contemporary garden with a Mediterranean feel. White was a favourite colour and they liked clean lines and decking. They wanted the design to include a water feature, but not a pond that would be unsafe for children.

The Brief

The clients wanted to create an elegant grown-up garden that was also suitable for the children. The design needed to address the slope and solve the bomb shelter dilemma. Laurence removed the overlooking window of the main bedroom and replaced it with glass doors and a balconette, so the view from upstairs was crucial to the design.

Outdoor lounge

It's not uncommon to find existing structures in the gardens of period houses. The options are to remove them, which can be costly and time consuming; to disguise them with judicious planting; or to use them as a stylish or practical resource.

The bomb shelter, which, on close examination turned out to be a well-constructed, concrete subterranean cube, could have been regarded as a white elephant. It was an original World War II bomb shelter, completely intact and of good solid shape. The squareness of the structure fitted well into the clean lines of the new design, and so the possibility of converting it from a dark bunker into an outdoor lounge emerged.

The idea was simple – to cut through the concrete lid leaving a lip all round, to remove the lid and replace with walls, roof and glass. This sort of construction and improvement work has many financial and engineering considerations and it's not something you should undertake lightly. Always consult an expert to make sure the proposed changes and means of undertaking them are safe.

On completion, the interior was treated very simply by being painted white. The result was a stylish room that could also act as a conservatory, capped with toughened glass. Its renovation added enormously to the contemporary feel of the garden and stood as a bright symbol of better times.

Planting

Gardens containing large or complex structures benefit enormously from considered planting. Where modern style is paramount, your choice of material should follow through. So a scheme based on a select few dramatic specimens with much use of ground cover was developed.

Exotic plants were the perfect answer – they are both dramatic and fashionable. A grass tree, *Xanthorrhoea australis*, was to be the main focal point; a spectacular plant that takes 100 years to grow just a metre of trunk, it was not an inexpensive option.

above *Tamarix tetrandra*, or Tamarisk, makes an exotic half-standard hedge, while looking elegant against glazed walling and white deck.

It was planted in the open glass room so that, although reasonably hardy, it would benefit from the extra protection.

The Blue palmetto, *Sabal palmetto*, a hardy palm with grand, fan-shaped leaves, was also included. Hardy enough to withstand British winters with some shelter, it was the perfect plant for the former bunker, not least because it grows slowly and was unlikely to reach the glass ceiling too quickly.

A large, sculptural *Agave americana* was planted to the side of the deck; it is hardy enough to live outside, but it does need good drainage and a sheltered spot. Although beautiful to look at, agaves do have hard, sharp spines at the leaf tips that are dangerous for children (and pets) if they are planted at their eye level.

Variegated ivy was bedded in as ground cover in the glass room, to soften the effect of the hard materials, and clumps of arum lilies, *Zantedeschia aethiopica* 'Crowborough', added their stunning flowers to the dramatic planting scheme, and reflected the white theme of the garden.

Colour

Colour can be introduced into the garden in many ways: through planting, paint effects, or the choice of materials.

There is a vogue for white in contemporary garden design and, in this brief, the clients expressed a love of the colour and requested that it be the basis of the design. You should, however, consider the benefits and drawbacks carefully before using it. White looks fantastic in bright sunshine, but in winter it can be cold and unwelcoming. In practical terms, it may not be the best colour because it inevitably gets dirty and requires repeated maintenance to keep it dazzling.

Here, the white decks made a definitive contrast with lush green planting and the lawn. The slightly tinted glass added colour and sparkle to the white decks and concrete, even on dull days.

top left Cool sophistication continues in the garden with clumps of arum lilies, *Zantedeschia aethiopica* 'Crowborough' adding their white flowers to the scheme.

top middle A 1960s coloured seat provides a flourish of colour.

top right The white stone and palm fronds create a Mediterranean feel.

above An elegant steel and glass table combined with aluminium cafe-style seating is the perfect furniture for the style-conscious gardener.

A LOOK AT THE DETAILS

 Agaves look great in this design. They have such a strong, bold shape and really stand out against the pale stones and decking. Incredibly tolerant of dry conditions, they are easy to look after, requiring very little water, even on hot summer days. But watch out for those hard spines on the tips of the leaves!

 To complete the idea of the outdoor lounge, the bunker was fitted with a television. This enclosed room now provided an alternative living room, where the clients could spend evenings in the garden all year round, either watching the television, or simply observing the stars above through the glass roof.

 I fell in love with this glass table and these chairs. They cried out to be placed in a contemporary scheme and were perfectly in keeping with the simple, uncluttered, glass theme of this design.

 The pink flowers of the *Tamarix tetrandra* keep to the simple theme of the garden but add a touch of delicate glamour and seasonal interest too.

 Gabions remind me of giant Lego bricks. You can do almost anything with them and they're brilliant for building retaining walls. Construction is a bit like building a dry-stone wall; you need smooth faces to the front and pack them densely to avoid holes. The metal mesh and cubist form have an industrial quality, but the variations in colour and shape of the stones are also very natural.

 Steps were essential in this garden because it was built on different levels, but I tried to keep them as essentially simple as the rest of the design. They were white and were faced with rough stone slabs to echo the stone within the gabions.

THE DESIGN

Opportunities for foreign travel have become commonplace today, and many of us have begun to bring back exotic influences to both house and garden. We often discover ways of living that make us feel comfortable in another culture. Taking an essence from your trips abroad can be an exciting source of new ideas for your scheme and reinterpreting it to create something that fits with your way of life can lead to a unique and creative design. However, the main fear is that by just copying and transporting influences you will create a foreign themeland.

In her design brief to me, Vina had included objects and photographs which displayed a rural African influence – buildings with thatched roofs, small pebbles and pieces of stone. I wanted to avoid creating an over-themed look, because any new design should be appropriate to its site and situation. The finished plan took Vina's desires for natural materials, plants and water and translated these into a garden that had a surprising oriental influence. A natural stone patio outside the house led to a straight walkway of wooden decking. Beyond this, our focal point was a pavilion that was built in a still pool of water to enhance its tranquillity.

above Wooden deck and large boulders combined with a still pond, help to create a natural setting.

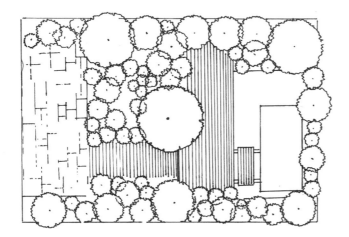

a good indication of how much she enjoyed her garden.

The Plot

The house was in a suburban area full of trees, shrubs and the sound of birdsong. Because the back garden was not overlooked, it had a feel of being a retreat. There was not a great deal of sun in the garden – only the part furthest away from the house attracted sunlight. There were many existing plants on the site, including five large lilac bushes, which Vina hated.

The Client

Vina was a very busy lady who lived alone and had a well-organized professional life. Previously, difficulties with builders had left her feeling distant from her half-finished home and reluctant to use it as a place in which to socialize. Her garden, however, was her refuge. Here, she enjoyed relaxing and growing plants, and her collection of gardening books was

The Brief

Vina wanted a garden which would focus on plants. The new design was to include a multipurpose retreat – an enclosed space that could be used for work, gardening and relaxation. She loved water and natural materials and was not afraid of maintenance. She wanted a place to escape and relax, surrounded by nature, and a site outdoors where she could, at last, entertain her friends.

right The pavilion is built around four green oak posts which travelled through the building down to the bottom of the pond.

Room for retreat

To have a place to escape to – a haven – is a common fantasy, especially for city dwellers. Your garden can contain a version of this – a room outside surrounded by plants and water. Providing shade from the sun or shelter from the rain, this can be a great place to enjoy the garden. If it's architecturally interesting, it can also form a perfect focal point.

In recent years, modern computing and communications technology have made it possible for many people to work from home, and this has given fresh impetus to the creation of new working environments that are separate from the house.

far right All of the windows to the front of the building are in fact floor-to-ceiling hinged doors.

top right Old dustbins are converted to form islands of marginal planting set into the still pond.

bottom right A wooden stepping stone crosses the still water.

But such work-places benefit enormously from being multifunctional – total enjoyment is key.

Vina's room was designed to act as a potting shed, a leisure retreat, an office and also a beautiful focal point. It was a simple wooden building constructed on four green-oak posts in the middle of a large pool. As it was constructed in wood and was relatively small in scale, it passed under planning regulations as a temporary structure.

Architecturally, it was simple and contemporary. The six glass doors and large side window were hung with wooden blinds that could be drawn down to the floor. Wired for electricity and computers, Vina could comfortably work here, and a simple stove ensured an even temperature throughout the year.

Water

Water can be used in the garden in many different ways and for many different reasons. Here it was used to create a peaceful, serene atmosphere and to put some distance between the pavilion and the house. To complete the idea of a hideaway – and to ensure total separation from both house and garden – the retreat was designed to sit on columns in a large rectangular pool. Despite the building being an elaborate construction, it achieved a lightness of touch that fitted well into this garden – the water travelled underneath and around it, forming a moat around her new studio. This also gave plenty of protection and shade to the goldfish that we introduced.

Vina had been keen to introduce moving water into

left and above Natural stone paving combined with a catwalk of decking and squared blocks of planting creates an overall feeling of simplicity. This is further enhanced by furniture constructed from railway sleepers.

the garden, but I felt that the stillness of a calm pool was more beneficial to relaxation – the addition of moving water in a relatively confined space can be distracting. The large pool created a sense of wonder and intrigue and acted as a mirror to reflect the planting and the building above.

Water features and ponds offer the opportunity to introduce a range of spectacular plants that would not otherwise find a home in your garden. Like any plant, the site and conditions in which they are planted are important. Still-water ponds provide the perfect situation for beautiful plants such as water lilies, which don't like moving water.

To plant the pond, we recycled old dustbins which we drilled with holes and filled with a mixture of stone, soil and charcoal. Filled with aquatic plants, such as *Caltha palustris* (kingcups), and *Typha minima*, these formed damp islands on the surface of the pool. Oxygenating plants beneath and a little duckweed floating on the surface completed the picture and established a healthy ecosystem in which the fish would thrive.

To provide access to the studio across the moat, we built a step from the decking that was used over the rest of the garden.

The pond was designed with a strictly formal outline to emphasize that we were not trying to pretend it had been naturally formed. It echoed the symmetrical lines of the garden as a whole, and was balanced by a rectangular deck for entertaining that emerged from the boundary wall.

A LOOK AT THE DETAILS

 Cherry blossoms are the cheerful harbingers of spring. In Japan, cherry blossom is highly prized and is symbolic of youth and regeneration. It is seen as part of the seasons changing throughout the year, reminding us of time passing.

 Large stones play a vital part in Japanese gardens. They are carefully placed to provide focal points and are used singularly or in groups. The large stone, in repose by the pavilion is a static form, which implies that the area is one for relaxation and contemplation.

 Variegated plants, such as hostas, irises and phormiums, bring an element of light and shade into the garden in imitation of the dappled shade of large trees. I also like these plants for their bold leaves – the sword-shaped foliage of iris and phormium instantly catch the eye in contrast with the more subtle, broader leaves of the hostas.

 Ferns and bog plants add to the lush greenness of this garden. Ferns are dotted in amongst other plants, particularly *Osmunda regalis* – called the Royal fern for its large, elegant fronds.

 Wooden decking and stone paving was used in this garden to reflect Vina's desire for natural materials. The pale-coloured flooring help to create a sense of tranquillity and peace, with brighter, but nevertheless subtle, colours introduced through the planting.

 The wooden pavilion is the central focus of the garden. This is a space for peaceful contemplation. It is made from green oak – green meaning that it has been freshly cut, not seasoned and will last a lifetime, even when submerged in water.

out
SPACE FOR THE KIDS

above A small, grassy mound combined with a curved, blue-painted wall and a lollipop tree create a playful feel for this family garden.

THE DESIGN

When dealing with a predominantly square or rectangular site, sweeping curves, ovals and circles work well to create excitement and interest and to draw the eye away from rigid outlines. Merline was a fan of Charles Jencks' cosmic Scottish garden – a landscape contoured into strange but beautiful, undulating mounds of turf. Taking inspiration

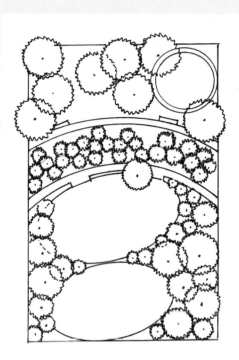

The Client

Merline was in her thirties, the single parent of three children. Having recently moved, she wanted to create the perfect family home and enjoy her first garden.

The Plot

Her good-sized, rectangular plot faced south. The large lawn was surrounded by borders that contained some mature shrubs and old-fashioned herbaceous planting. A small, slab-concrete patio ran alongside the house, which, despite being neo-Georgian, was undistinguished when viewed from the rear.

The Brief

The design for this garden was definitely to be child-orientated. Merline disliked the traditional look, and wanted a stimulating, contemporary, fun place, a den for her teenage son and an area where she could sit, watch the children and read. She adored bright colours and boldly architectural planting styles. She loved curves and her ideal garden would contain mounds of grass.

from this and the set of the children's television programme *Teletubbies*, I designed an oval lawn that included a small, grassy mound.

The main feature of the garden was a huge curved wall, planted with grasses on top, and incorporating small tunnels for the children to run through. An oval cobbled patio near the house was designed for adult relaxation and the back of the garden was devoted to a children's climbing frame, a circular den and a small plantation of trees.

Gardens for children

It's very important to take every member of the family into consideration when planning your plot. If there are children around, the design can be geared towards them without creating simply an obviously juvenile playground. A garden may undergo many changes of style and use over the years, and a feature that was originally created for children, such as a sunken sandpit, could easily evolve into a pond as they grow older and wiser.

You may, however, decide that the children should have ownership of the complete plot to create their own spaces for dens and football, and that you will reclaim the space for planting and relaxation when their interests and preoccupations have moved on. If you are going to wait for a more suitable time to develop your idea of paradise, plant up a background that will survive the rigours of junior life. By establishing climbers against the walls and planting a few specimen trees, you will be creating a good framework to build on in the future. On the other hand, you could create a space exclusively for the kids as part of your overall design and make a physical divide within your garden that will give them some privacy.

Merline wanted to make a strong statement with this garden; one that would be obviously contemporary and not necessarily child-based in future years. So the curved wall did the job of raising the planting to a good, safe height, while also acting as a sculpture. A feature like this adds an air of mystery and, because its circular apertures invite the viewer to explore, both children and adults will be tempted by curiosity to discover what lies beyond.

Space for the children

When creating an area for children, there are some major considerations to bear in mind. Safety is paramount and should be integral to your thinking when planning the space and the activities that will go on there. You need to create a safe space where you know that you needn't worry about them. If you want to put in a climbing frame with swings and ropes, as I did here, make sure that all equipment is properly installed and regularly checked for wear and tear. If the children's play area is going to be visible from the rest of the garden, you might want to consider wooden play things, because wood blends in much more easily in a garden than garish, brightly-coloured plastics. If you do decide to go for wood, check it regularly to make sure it is free of splinters. Children are prone to falling, so it is important to think about surface finishing material. Play bark is now widely available and is a good flooring for children, because it absorbs impact. An alternative is washed sand, but beware of neighbouring cats, who may leave undesirable deposits; a material like this should be covered when not in use.

Water can be included in a children's garden for their entertainment, but it must be safe as even the smallest depth can be dangerous. Fountains that operate by means of water recirculated via safely covered reservoirs will be a delight.

Older children can discover different joys in the garden and, as inside the house, they look for private spaces – places where adults are not allowed. Darren, Merline's son, wanted a place where he could entertain his friends, well away from younger siblings. A cylindrical structure was built of wood and painted purple. It was a place to watch television, play computer games, or do homework throughout the year.

Space for the adults

Remember to include somewhere for the adults. Usually this will be a place to sit and relax or entertain. In this garden we included a cobbled area where the previous

patio had been. The cobbles were wired together in patterns and laid on sand, in an oval shape of similar proportions to the lawn.

Planting

Children like to be surrounded by plants too, but the planting plan will have different criteria from that of a garden predominantly for adults. In general, avoid thorns, spikes and prickles unless they are well out of harm's way; they can do serious damage. There are plants that are beautiful to look at, but danger lurks beneath for enquiring hands and mouths. The most common ones are plants with poisonous berries, such as yew; sappy ones, like euphorbia or *Ruta graveolens* (rue) which can irritate skin and eyes; and those in which all parts are toxic, such as the foxglove, *Digitalis purpurea*. It's worthwhile investigating how child-friendly a plant is before you buy.

Children instinctively reach out and touch, so try to incorporate textures into their space that they will enjoy.

Anything soft and furry, like the aptly-named Lamb's ears (*Stachys byzantina*), is always a favourite. Lawns make a great playing surface and will cushion the inevitable falls, but choose a sturdy amenity mix of grass seed that will withstand the wear and tear. Ornamental grasses can also be a good choice. In this garden we used a range of different grasses on top of the wall – *Carex buchananii*, *Miscanthus sinensis*, and *Stipa arundinacea*; the different heights, textures and colours of their foliage looked wonderful against the crisp backdrop of the blue wall. We also used a specimen bay tree (*Laurus nobilis*), whose lollipop head echoed other circle shapes in the garden and softened the appearance of the wall. Some plants such as the Chusan palm *Trachycarpus fortunei*, the tree fern *Dicksonia antarctica*, and *Fatsia japonica*, combine a sense of fun and sophistication. But don't be precious about your garden; delicate herbaceous treasures will get battered by footballs and brightly coloured flowers will prove irresistible to curious little hands.

A LOOK AT THE DETAILS

Painted walls, fences and structures always benefit from the cooling effect of greenery, and this bay tree (*Laurus nobilis*) helps to tone down the vibrant blue wall. Blue looks great in the summer and introduces much needed colour in the dark grey days of winter.

Children love the soft furry bark of the *Trachycarpus fortunei*, or the Chusan windmill palm. It is a reliably hardy palm but it's not mad keen on bitter east winds which burn its leaves, so it is much happier in a sheltered spot if possible.

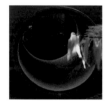
Big industrial concrete pipes will provide hours of amusement for the kids, and are perfect for providing an exciting tunnel into their play area. Raw materials such as these will also be a good deal cheaper than any designed children's features.

Grasses are very much the plants of the moment. Fashionable, low maintenance and naturalistic, they add instant effect and drama to any planting scheme.

The portholes in the den echo the circular window which is a feature of the house's architecture and also enhance the hideaway nature of the den.

The Tasmanian tree fern or *Dicksonia antarctica* is an old favourite of mine. Its lush foliage and jungle-like appearance create a sense of mystery. It is a plant that fits in with a garden like this one, as both adults and children will love it.

out A 'HANGING' GARDEN

above A circular lawn is speckled with slabs of concrete and glass which are underlit with fibre optics.

THE DESIGN

The solution here needed to escape the boundaries, even if this meant creating new ones. I designed a circular wall to create a comfortable inner sanctum that would hold the eye within it. Beside the house and at the end of the garden, the walls were double-skinned, to allow for planting at a height. Plants would cascade from the top of the walls, softening the white-rendered surface, while also diverting attention from the high-rise building across the road. We installed a gate, which could be closed to separate off a safe area for Flora, and a large, circular aperture in the wall formed an opening through which the family could keep an eye on her. The raised beds would also be 2m (6ft) tall, to protect plants from Flora's mischief.

The main flooring was turf with inlaid concrete and glass slabs, underlit with multi-coloured, fibre optic lighting. But along the awkward alleyway that led from the living room, more traditional hard landscaping was used. Yellow and brown clay pavers were laid in a diamond pattern, with planting at ground level against the boundary walls, to create a view from the kitchen window for whoever was on washing-up duty.

Finally, a den for Kyle was built at the rear of the garden, to give him personal space to enjoy with friends.

Garden construction

Creating large garden structures should never be undertaken without consulting the relevant planning authorities. Specialist assistance is always recommended for electrical installations or complicated construction.

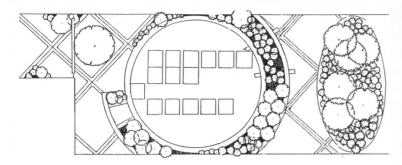

The Clients

Jim and Katherine are a fun loving couple who had recently moved to a terraced Georgian house in Northampton. Their energetic and friendly son Kyle was in his early teens, while their beautiful daughter Flora was severely autistic with no speech and very challenging behaviour and needed constant supervision.

The Plot

The house was a Grade II listed building which would have a big impact on designs for both house and garden. The garden was small and other than a chalet-style wooden shed was featureless. The background to the garden was an ugly multi-storey car park.

The Brief

Jim and Katherine loved design and the requirements for their plot were multi-faceted. Despite Flora's difficulties they did not want to compromise and play safe with garden style. Within the relatively small enclosure they wanted to create big impact. Of prime concern however, were Flora's difficulties. Previous attempts at gardening had ended in failure as she was prone to pull up flowers, eat soil and throw loose debris, such as stones, over the garden wall. It was obvious that good humour and tolerance were virtues bestowed on her parents, so it was important that the design should match these virtues. The garden should be stimulating and entertaining, different to the norm, and have a wow factor, but should also be one where the family could relax, sit outside, enjoy a meal, read a newspaper and have some peace. The garden should engage Flora but be suitable and safe for her needs.

above Circular holes in the curved wall house projectors which beam favourite images from slides around the garden.

left The main planting in our modern garden is contained in giant troughs on top of the curved walls.

above Two copper pipes shoot water out from the top beds.

left A traditional circular opening leads from one part of the garden into another. The walk-through to the car park is seen in the distance.

Before any of this work proceeds, you must make sure that you are not contravening any planning regulations. This is especially true in a conservation area, or if your house has some form of statutory protection. This house was Grade II listed, so consent was needed for anything that might change the character of the house, or the garden. Planning permission was sought and, after recommendations by the council were taken into account and modifications made, we were given the all clear to proceed. If you don't get the relevant permission, you can be required by law to reverse your work.

Flora's activity room
While researching Flora's autism, we discovered that colour can be stimulating for people with learning difficulties, so we used fibre-optic technology to create multi-coloured lighting effects beneath the glass slabs in the lawn. In reality, this created fun for the whole family and visitors alike; they all admired the twinkling colours.

Built into the circular walls, sealed safely behind clear glass, projectors beamed pictures of Flora's and Kyle's favourite images across the 'room' at three separate points. A remote control allowed mum and dad to change the images and to decorate the outdoor gallery with pictures of Disney characters, elephants and fish.

An outdoor shower that projected water from two copper pipes was installed to satisfy Flora's fondness for water. Again, this was used under parental supervision and both the water source and collecting reservoirs with submersible pumps were safely out of reach.

Planting
In this garden, we had to accommodate Flora's special needs without function compromising the design's

above Bamboo was planted in the patio area to soften the walls and paving all year round.

right Near the house, more traditional paving set in diagonal squares and old brick walls create a more homely style.

aesthetic appeal, and so some imaginative solutions had to come into play.

Here, planting had to be well away from prying hands so the circular walls became raised beds, albeit very high ones. Because the space beneath the beds was to be used for storage and a room for Kyle, the construction had to be watertight. By means of a heavy-duty pond liner and a sophisticated drainage system, the beds became self-contained troughs, filled with a mix of soil and compost to a depth of 30cm (1ft). The weight of this, considerable when wet, was supported by hidden beams. As in any raised beds or containers, plants dry out more quickly than those in open ground. So we installed an automatic irrigation system with an inbuilt timer.

Without planting, the walls of Flora's room and the steel grid pergola that linked them with Kyle's den would have appeared too brutal. Over the pergola,

I mingled an ornamental vine, *Vitis coignetiae*, with *Clematis armandii* 'Snowdrift', and planted *Wisteria floribunda* for its exquisite lilac flowers that would hang elegantly beneath bands of industrial steel.

In this garden, I felt it was important to maintain year-round colour to soften the stark white walls, so I used evergreens that remain the same throughout the year, and herbaceous plants that will fade away in winter. Some of my herbaceous favourites include *Astilbe* 'Aphrodite', with really beautiful pink flowers and ferny foliage, *Achillea* 'Moonshine', and creeping bugle, *Ajuga reptans. Cupressus sempervirens*, the Italian cypress, made a strong vertical impact on the planting scheme and, in this case, contrasted beautifully with the autumn hues of *Cercis canadensis* 'Forest Pansy'. *Carex buchananii*, a bronze-leaved sedge, and the bamboo, *Arundinaria gigantea* were used to provide further year-round interest.

A LOOK AT THE DETAILS

Large, plain mirrors were mounted on the walls at either end of the room so that Flora could be seen at all times and in all corners. Mirrors also perform a great trick in reflecting the surroundings, making a small area appear much larger than it actually is.

The contemporary pergola was made from steel concrete-reinforcing grids; it linked the space between the circular room and the den at the rear of the garden. The pergola allows planting to cascade down from above, and also linked with planting in the raised beds of the double wall.

These simple copper pipes were set high up in the wall, safely out of reach. The pipes pour water down inside the room and function as an entertainment for Flora as well as a practical outdoor shower.

These concrete slabs were inlaid with glass bricks, through which shone coloured fibre optics to create a disco-effect floor. Fibre optics are easy to install and once fitted are virtually maintenance free. The light travels along glass fibres, as fine as human hair, which are bundled together like electric cables. They are very safe, since they carry no dangerous electricity or heat.

The shower poured into a soakaway, which channelled the flow so that the ground didn't get slippery and unsafe. It was made from a blend of recycled truck tyres and glue and applied to a grate above the reservoir tank. A porous material – dyed green to blend in with the lawn – was then laid on top of this.

The pure white wall was a perfect backdrop to some vibrant planting. The *Photinia* x *fraseri* 'Red Robin' looked stunning against the white, and is unusual because its juvenile foliage is red, maturing to green. Its spherical crown also brilliantly echoed the circular shapes in the garden.

out A 'BRIDGET JONES' GARDEN

above From the house only the outdoor living area is visible. There's no hint of the outside sunken area – this is only seen when you are lured through the garden, enticed by the sight of the vivid gold pyramid.

THE DESIGN

Privacy is often top of a client's wish list. While it can be impractical, or even impossible, to screen off your garden completely, a sense of seclusion can be achieved in a variety of ways.

One solution is to excavate to create somewhere snug and cosy, out of sight from ground or fence level. For this garden, this was part of the solution. The design answer seemed to me to create two diamond-shaped areas, one a sunken lounge for the times when Sharon wanted privacy, the other, a decked, outdoor dining area at ground level at the rear of her kitchen – for ease of entertaining. A large railway-sleeper table was built to fulfil the entertainment brief, and stepping stones made from decking linked all the features in the garden.

The sunken lounge was surrounded by raised beds to enhance the effect of depth. The golden pyramid was used as a focal point and placed within the raised beds. The sunken area was not immediately visible to wandering visitors, but the pyramid commanded attention, demanding closer inspection, which, in turn, revealed the surprise at its base.

My approach to this plot was to use strong horizontal and vertical lines, but Sharon was keen on introducing curves, so I blurred the distinction by blunting the sharp corners of the shapes with planting and rounding off the edges of the decks and steps.

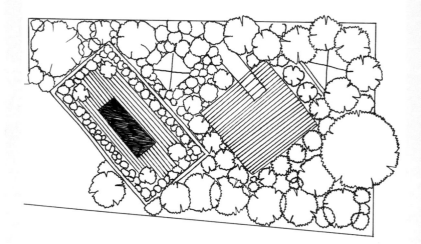

could come and enjoy with her as well as an area where she could relax on her own after a busy day at work and feel secure and content. The garden was only concerned with Sharon's happiness.

The Plot

The garden was a flat, rectangular plot carpeted by a neglected lawn and a few forlorn shrubs on either side. Sharon and her garden could never share quality time alone as it was overlooked by high risers.

The Client

Sharon was a thirty-something, career woman who lived alone. Attached to her flat was a very large suburban garden which she didn't understand. It was boring with no redeemable features. She would visit it occasionally, hugging the edges for security. The relationship was not a good one. As a couple, she and the garden needed guidance. What she wanted was a place that her friends

The Brief

The design should provide a psychological break from her hectic office life. It was to be sleek, stylish, pink and curvy and somewhere Sharon could go out in summer or winter and feel at peace. It was to have a relationship with the concept of interior living and to provide spaces for eating, drinking and lounging. It was to be given a heart, a glittery Barbie one.

Sunken lounge

A feeling of protection and security was an important part of this brief, so the design of the sunken room was appealing. To create her 'lounge', major excavation work was needed. We dug out a two-metre deep rectangular pit and poured in concrete footings. The hole was then lined with concrete blocks. Drainage is important in any space that is so deep beneath ground level, and here we incorporated a shaft and sump pump so that the recessed area did not immediately turn into a sunken pond with the first shower.

Plain decking was introduced as a flooring material and the concrete blocks were rendered and painted – orange. This may seem a garish choice but when you consider that Sharon's social life revolved around funky clubs and pubs this décor appealed to her. However, this orange paint – which was also subsequently adorned with discs of mirror-finished stainless steel –

left The sunken lounge screams kitsch.

left While planting tumbles in from the raised beds above, a complete air of privacy has been created by digging down into the garden. Simple furniture on castors can be rearranged at a moment's notice, and lighting boxes, complete with VW Beetle headlamps, can be left outside all year round.

could not be seen from the rest of the relatively serene garden.

Powerful lighting was provided for the room by Volkswagen Beetle headlamps. These were set into boxes made from decking which were placed on the floor and on top of one another. In the garden above the room, spot lights led the way safely back to the house.

As it was below ground level, the room was sheltered from the wind, but a large outdoor gas heater ensured warmth, even in winter. The 'room' was made to feel more like an interior too by including movable furniture units that could double as daybeds or seats, a coffee table, and a power supply for a stereo or television set.

Planting

One side of the garden was already planted with Leyland cypress. All too often these fast-growing conifers are seen as a panacea for privacy concerns, but they frequently create more problems than they solve. These plants may block the neighbours' sight lines into the garden, but they also dramatically reduce light coming in to it. They are also very boring to look at, as well as being heavy feeders and drinkers, so that it becomes a struggle for anything growing near them to compete. That said, if you have the time to keep them well clipped, they can make elegant formal hedges.

In this case, we removed all but one Leyland. The survivor would provide some height until the new plants matured; the height was much needed to break

right An outdoor dining area is furnished with a table to seat ten, simply made from four sand-blasted railway sleepers placed on a metal frame.

up the line of buildings that overlooked the garden from all sides.

A combination of easy-maintenance planting was used to soften the severe lines of the rendered concrete and the diamond-shaped outlines of the sunken room and dining area.

Sharon's favourite colour was pink, so I had a challenge to introduce this into the garden. Paint will always brighten up a garden, especially in the winter, and planting can add more varied shades in the summer. So I used a warm pink paint, similar to the one used by Laurence in the kitchen, to enhance the wall of a low raised bed and ensure a year-round presence of pink. I also used plants to create a pink paradise, including campanulas, *Abelia*, *Spiraea* and geraniums.

Large bamboos can hold the eye within the garden and add real drama, as well as a soothing rustle in the breeze. Running bamboos can spread madly and may be hard to control, so go for clumping forms, such as *Fargesia nitida* or *F. murielae*, if space is restricted. *Dicksonia antarctica* is the most wonderful tree fern for instant impact and, here, it helped to melt the pyramid structure into the ground. Bronze-leaved grasses and orange-flowered azaleas picked up the colour of the

sunken lounge below. A large eucalyptus, with amazing blue-green foliage all year round and interesting bark that peeled to reveal a range of subtle shades, took the bare look off the massive brick wall; because it was a listed structure, we could not cover it with trellis and climbing plants.

Sharon is an excellent cook and loved giving dinner parties, so we planted a large herb garden around the dining area. The theme was continued between the decking stepping stones so that, as she brushed past them, the herbs released a fabulous scent. In this part of the garden, we planted some culinary herbs, including sage, *Salvia officinalis*, and variegated apple mint, *Mentha suaveolens* 'Variegata', and other aromatic ones, like the chamomile, *Chamaemelum nobile*, and the curry plant, *Helichrysum italicum*.

Herbs generally like to have a fair bit of room for their roots, but prefer a fairly poorish soil, so don't feed them too much. Invasive herbs, as their name suggests, will take over your plot given half the chance, so contain villains, such as mint, in pots. If you want them in the ground with your other herbs, sink the pot into the ground instead. Leave the pot rim about 5cm (2in) above soil level to prevent them escaping.

A LOOK AT THE DETAILS

 The simple shape of the golden pyramid really stimulated interest. The suburban equivalent of a folly, it was cheaply and easily constructed using exterior quality marine plywood. The resulting form can be left plain, or painted, as here, or clad in sheet copper, aluminium or stainless steel.

 Sharon wanted to be able to use her private sunken room day and night. So we installed adaptable furniture units on wheels that could be moved around to follow the sun by day, doubling up as comfortable seating or a place to recline by night.

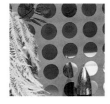 Stainless steel discs were fixed to the walls of the sunken lounge for a nightclub ambience. They also softened the effect of the bright orange paint and provided a wonderful surface to reflect light, like a huge, disco mirror ball.

 The large dining table was made of four reclaimed railway sleepers laid on a metal frame; their weight meant that they didn't have to be attached to it in any way. It's best to try to find new sleepers rather than reclaimed ones, since new ones won't contain creosote, or leak tar on a hot day.

 These lights in boxes were made from the same decking that we used for the floor. They were inset with Volkswagen Beetle headlamps to create fun, durable lighting. The boxes could be moved around the room to vary their effect, or stacked on top of each other. They could even be used as extra seating if needed.

 To provide access to the sunken lounge, we installed concrete steps. They are very durable and have the advantage that they don't become slippery when wet, as decking often does. They also need minimal maintenance.

ACKNOWLEDGEMENTS

Much gratitude from Laurence to Rachel Innes-Lumsden and Franny Moyle who started the whole thing off. Gordon Whistance and Pamela Winstanley and Fletcher in the BBC Art Department. Pia Munden, the ever-present representative of Llewelyn-Bowen Ltd and the companies whose involvement, time and resources were invaluable. Every member of the design and construction team over the last four series. Not forgetting, of course, our esteemed participants without whose gardens and rooms we'd have no series.

Thanks from Diarmuid to Laurence, for being such fun. To Jane Root, Owen Gay, Franny Moyle, Rachel Innes-Lumsden and Ben McPherson for letting the two of us go mad.

To Jim, Catherine, Flora and Kyle for showing us what it's all about. To Stuart Sharpless for saying 'I built that' and to Amanda de Ryk who puts up with us and continues to strive for designs. To John Ferguson for creating with such good humour.

For the book: Nicky Copeland for dedication and perseverance. To Helena Caldon who was inspirational in her commitment to create a beautiful book. Robin and Alice Wood for a night at the races! Justine Keane whose perspiration created the framework and whose love makes a home. To Paul Vater and Robin Matthews for their wonderful design and photographs.

To my team John, Polly, Debbie, Kathryn and Brian at John Noel Management – thanks for all the help over the years. Special thanks to Nik Linen for looking after me so well.

Thanks to Joan, Jack, Declan, Niamh, Emer, David, Gerry, Ronan, Terry, Madeleine, Jane, Karl, Tim, Natasha, Julia, Holly, Ben, Yayee, Wendy O'Connalaigh, Tom Curran, Vincent Barnes, Bernard O'Rourke, Barry Cotter, Sean Keirghan, Anita Notaro, Pat Dixon, Vicky Jebb, Pat, Jane, Eilis, Rory, Niall, Renee and the Mannings in Liverpool, Susan, baby Jack, Rebecca and bump!

Thanks from both of us to our directors who are so much fun: Dan Adamson, Amelia Dare, Dave Smith, Anna Gravelle, Nadia Haggar, Ed Bazalgette, Andy Devonshire, Christian Digby, Micci Billinger, Stuart, Pete Leonard, Ann Wilson, Randal Wright, Helen Foulkes.

To Johnny Dobbyn, Charles Ponniah, Liam Barran, Rob Green, Dave Eaves, Damon Brown, Tony Gardener, Dean and Jason Harvey, Branton Bamford, Geoff Allen, Neil Pike, Padraig Sullivan, Terence O'Flaherty, Emma Brown, Jenny Cole, Barry Dickson, Misty Gale, Wendy Bawden, Andrea Hayes, Josie Milani, Jackie Ramsamy, Ed Robinson, Tim Fransham, Jacqueline Toon, John Briner, Richard Burton, Richard Cane, Tessa Carey, Cynthia Charles, Barry Dixon, Raewyn Dickson, Barbara Gibson, Deborah Harry, Alison Hollies, Lucy Hooper, Seb Illis, Zoe Ingham, Anna Lukashuk, Trupti Magecha, Paul Middleton, Eden Palm, Jules Pownell, Julie Stephenson, Hannah Wesson, Gordon Whistance, Sengul Bobbin, Robert Kershaw, John Lister, Lucyina Moodie, Ruth Miller, Blue Ryan, Matthew Stonehouse, Judi Wild Howe, Geraint Davies, Sarah Granger, Fergus Meiklejohn, Jane Moore, Richard Parkin, Caroline Tummons, Sue Banks, Lindi Day, Maggi Gibson, Alison Reynolds, Linda Stephens, Ryan Eltermon, Shana Williams, Leceia Gordon, Sophie Dyas, Craig Hunter, Jay, Derek Orpen, Emma Stevenson.

COMPLETE SUPPLIERS LIST

Interiors

APPLIANCES

Ariston
Tel: 0870 901 1090

Asko
Tel: 01275 3430001895

Atag
Tel: 01275 877 301
e-mail: info@atag.co.uk
www.atag.co.uk

Blanco
Oxgate Lane,
London NW2 7JN
Tel: 020 8452 3399

Caradon Plumbing Solutions
Stockists 0870 840 1000

Coolectric Ltd (Liebherr)
Tel: 01977 665 665
www.lhg.liebherr.com

DR Cookerhoods Ltd
Tel: 01252 515 355
www.cookerhoods.net

Maurice Lay Distributors Ltd
Tel: 0117 938 1900
www.mlay.co.uk

Miele Company Ltd
Fair Acres, Marcham Rd
Abingdon, Oxfordshire
OX14 ITW
Tel: 01235 554 455

Morso Stoves
Tel: 0121 386 6306
www.morsostoves.co.uk

Neff
Grand Union House,
Old Wolverton Rd,
Wolverton, Milton Keynes,
Bucks MK12 5PT
Tel: 01908 328 300
www.neff.co.uk

Servis
Tel: 0121 568 8555

Smeg
Tel: 0870 843 7373
www.smeguk.com

Zanussi
Tel: 0870 572 7727

BATHROOM

Hansgrohe
Tel: 01372 465 655
e-mail:
sales@hansgrohe.co.uk
www.hansgrohe.co.uk

Ideal Standard
The Bathroom Works
National Ave, Hull HU5 4IIS
Tel: 01482 346 461

Matki
Tel: 01454 322 888
e-mail: helpline@matki.cu.uk
www.matki.co.uk

Mira Realm
Stockists 0870 840 0035

Original Bathrooms
Tel: 020 8940 7554
e-mail:
fredhco@dircon.co.uk

Thermal Reflections
Tel: 0191 520 1503
e-mail: thermal.reflections
@virgin.net

Triton
Tel: 0800 0644 645
www.tritonshowers.co.uk

Twyfords and Caradon Plumbing Solutions
Lawton Rd, Alsager, Stoke
on Trent, Staffs ST7 2DF
Tel: 01270 879 777
www.caradon-plumbing.com

Ucosan
Tel: 01625 525 252
www.ucosan.nl

Villeroy & Boch
Tel: 020 8871 4028

BUILDING MATERIALS

Ally Tower Services Ltd
Tel: 020 8671
5277/5022/6277

Armfield Glass Ltd
191 Church Rd, Benfleet
Essex SS7 4PN
Tel: 01268 793 067

Aspinallis Building and Decorating Contractors
Tel: 020 8888 1692
e-mail: shaunaspinall@
fsmail.net
www.aspinallsuk.co.uk

Builders Beams
6-22 West St,
East Grinstead, W Sussex
Tel: 01342 301 501
www.builderbeams.co.uk

Champions
Tel: 020 8542 1606

Daedalian Glass
Tel: 01253 702 531
www.daedalian-glass.co.uk

C. Downhills Steels
Units C D & E
Riverside Way, Uxbridge
UB8 2YS
Tel: 01895 256 681

Trollope Colls Elliot Ltd
Tel: 0118 986 6668
www.skanska.co.uk.

James Latham Plc
Tel:020 8806 3333.

The Latvian Plywood Company
Tel: 01959 497017
www.latvianplywood

Marmox
Tel: 01634 828 461
www.marmox.com

M. Marcus Ltd
Tel: 01384 243 312
www.m-marcus.com

Robert May of Holloway Ltd
Tel: 020 7272 5225
www.robertmay.co.uk

MK Electrics
Tel: 01268 563 000
www.mkelectric.co.uk

The Pipeline Centre
Tel: 020 7394 2200

J. F. Ratcliff (Metals) Ltd
New Summer Street
Birmingham B19 3QN
Tel: 0121 359 5901
e-mail:
sales@jfratcliff.co.uk
www.jfratcliff.co.uk

J. D. Sign and Display
Tel: 020 8949 4468

The Stone Federation of Great Britain
Construction House,
56-64 Leonard St,
London EC2A 4JX
Tel: 020 7608 5094

Surrey Stainless Steel
Tel: 020 8684 9596

The Worldwide Wood Co Ltd
154 Colney Hatch Lane
Muswell Hill,
London N10 1ER
Tel: 0800 458 3366
e-mail: worldwidewood@
dial.pipex.com

DOORS AND WINDOWS

AB Construction (UK) Ltd
2 Little Malgraves
Ind Estate,
Upminster, Essex
RM14 3TE
Tel: 01268 410 810

Aspen Conservatories
Tel: 01992 710 500 for info

Clayton Munroe Ltd
Kingston West Drive,
Kingston, Staverton,
Totnes, Devon TQ9 6AR
Tel: 01803 762 626
e-mail:
mail@claytonmunroe.com
www.claytonmunroe.com

The Cotswold Casement Co.
Tel: 01608 605 568
www.cotswold-casements.co.uk

Haf Designs
Tel: 0800 389 8821
www.hafdesigns.co.uk

Dorma Glass
Tel: 01462 472 500
e-mail: glass@dorma-uk.co.uk

Focus Do It All
Tel. 0800 436 436
www.focusdoitall.co.uk

John Hardman Studios
Tel: 0121 429 7609

Holloway Products Ltd
Tel: 020 8594 4472
www.holloway-products.com

Philips
99 Portobello Rd, London
W11 2QB
www.neilphillips.co.uk

Rainbow Windows
Tel: 01621 744 744

The Sash Window Workshop
Tel: 0800 597 2598
e-mail:
sales@sashwindow.com

Senior Aluminium Systems
Unit 31, Burnt Mills
Industrial Estate,
Basildon, Essex SS13 1LT
Tel: 01268 725 720

SF Structural Glazing
Tel: 01322 290 555

CURTAINS/ BLINDS

Amari Plastics
Tel: 020 8961 1961

AMO Blinds & Fabrics Ltd
Tel: 01924 235 600
www.amoblinds.co.uk

Bamboo Harris Fabrics Ltd
Tel: 01908 366 977

Briant Curtaining
e-mail:
BRIANT@waverider.co.uk

WG Lucas & Sons Ltd
Tel: 023 9282 6629
www.lucas-sails.com

Crest Leather
Tel: 020 8457 7129
www.crestleather.com

Crowson Fabrics
Tel: 01825 761 055
www.cre8tiv.com
/crowsonfabrics

Curtains Direct Ltd
Tel: 01268 779 955
e-mail: Design.Display
@btinternet.co.uk

Curtain Mania
Tel: 01784 245 417

The Curtain Clinic
Tel: 020 8767 2254
e-mail: curtain.clinic
@lineone.net

Wendy Cushing Trimmings
Tel: 020 8556 3555

Doreen Fitton
Tel: 01625 590 413

IKEA
www.ikea.co.uk

Luxaflex
Tel: 0161 432 5303

Marina Mill Ltd
Cuxton, Kent ME2 1AB
Tel: 01634 718 871

Monarch Knitting Machinery (UK) Ltd
74 Boston Rd,
Leicester LE4 1BG
Tel: 0116 235 1502
e-mail: general@
monarchknitting.co.uk
www.monarchknitting.co.uk

Next
Tel: 0845 600 7000
e-mail: www.next.co.uk

Peter the Pleater
Tel: 020 7375 1053

Pret a Vivre
Tel: 0845 130 5161
www.pretavivre.com

Soft Options
Tel: 01256 817 100
www.blinddesign.co.uk

Bernard Thorpe
Tel: 020 7352 5457

Universal Blind & Curtain Systems Ltd
Tel: 01727 875 533

Whaleys (Bradford) Ltd
Tel: 01274 576 718
www.whaleys-bradford.ltd.uk

FABRICS

G. P. & J. Baker
Tel: 01494 467 467

Beckford Silk Ltd
Tel: 01386 881 507
www.beckfordsilk.co.uk

Bennett Silks
Tel: 0161 476 8600
www.bennett-silks.co.uk

Bridge of Weir Leather Company Ltd
Tel: 01505 612 132
www.bowleather.co.uk

Angela Burgin Furnishing & Design Ltd
www.abfd.co.uk

Cambaz Yorganlar Frances Place
238 Dartford Rd, Dartford
Kent DA1 3EY
Tel: 0780 830 7133

Chase Erwin
Chelsea Design Centre
Chelsea Harbour, London
SW10 0XE
Tel: 020 7352 7271
e-mail: silk@chase-erwin.com
www.chase-erwin.com

Celia Birtwell
71 Westbourne Park Rd
London W2 5QH
Tel: 020 7221 0877

The Cloth House
98 Berwick St, Soho
London W1V 3PP
Tel: 020 7287 1555

Designs on U Ltd
Tel: 01625 430 077
www.corporatelogodirect.com

DFG
278-280 Brompton Rd
London SW3 2AS
Tel: 020 7589 4778

Dylon International Ltd
Tel: 020 8663 4801
www.dylon.co.uk

Kvadrat Ltd
Tel: 020 7229 9969
www.Kvadrat.dk

John Lewis
Tel: 020 7629 7711
www.johnlewis.com

Lynplan Ltd
Tel: 020 8681 1831
www.lynplan.com

Mulberry Home
Tel: 01202 575 457 for stockists

Osborne and Little
304-308 King's Rd,
London SW3
Tel: 020 7352 1456

Peacock Blue
Tel: 0870 333 1555
e-mail:
sales@peacockblue.co.uk

Pongees Ltd
Tel: 020 7739 9130
www.pongees.co.uk

Philippa Prinsloo
Tel: 07980 269 391
e-mail: prinsloophilippa
@hotmail.com

The Printworks
Tel: 0161 483 5200

Sanderson
Tel: 01895 830 000
www.sanderson-uk.com

Threadbare Upholstery
Tel: 023 8021 1721

FLOORING

Allied Carpets
Tel: 01689 895 000

Amtico
Tel: 0800 667 766
www.amtico.com

Bruce Hardwood Floors
Tel: 01235 515 102
www.bruce.com

The Carpet Studio
Tel: 0800 781 7882
www.thecarpetstudio.co.uk

Crucial Trading
Tel: 01562 820 006
e-mail: sales@crucial-trading.com

The Delabole Slate
Tel: 01840 212 242
www.delaboleslate.com

Floors by Design
Tel: 020 7384 3959
e-mail: ideas@
floorsbydesign.co.uk
www.floorsbydesign.co.uk

Floorstyles of Leominster
Tel: 01568 612 322
www.floorstyles.co.uk

Hard Rock Flooring
Tel: 01296 658 755
www.hardrockflooring.co.uk

Hill & Co
Tel: 01737 844 555
www.hillco.co.uk

Hornton Masonry C.
Edge Hill, Nr Banbury
Oxfordshire OX15 6DX.
Tel: 01295 670 238/670 750

Kersiant Cobb & Company
Tel: 01675 430 430

Kingsmead Carpets
Tel: 01290 421 511

John Myland Ltd
Tel: 020 8670 9161
www.mylands.co.uk

The Original Stone Company
Tel: 01332 374 812
www.theoriginalstoneco.uk

PTL Interiors Ltd
Tel: 020 8402 0900

Dennis Ruabon Ltd
Tel: 01978 843 484
www.dennisruabon.co.uk

Southern & Darwent
Tel: 0161 745 9287
www.southern-darwent.co.uk

Taz Timber Ltd
Tel: 01268 570 571
www.taz-timber.co.uk

Uzin Ltd
Tel: 01235 534 106

Wicanders
Tel: 01403 710 001
www.wicanders-amorim.co.uk

Woodrow Hardwood Flooring
Tel: 020 7228 5106
www.woodrow-hardwood-flooring.co.uk

FURNITURE

AC Buckoke & Sons Ltd
Tel: 020 7223 3746

Armoire Lindale and Chambers
Ddole Industrial Estate
Llandrindod,
Wales LD1 6DF
Tel: 01597 824 001

Artistic Engineers
Unit J, Atlas Business
Centre, Oxgate Lane,
London NW2 7HJ
Tel: 020 8450 2163

A Touch of Brass
Tel: 020 7352 5495

B&G Projects
Tel: 01923 825 812
www.bgprojects.co.uk

Bianchi Furniture
Tel: 01462 433 130
www.bianchifurniture.co.uk

California Closets
Tel: 0845 606 6063
e-mail: info@calclosets.co.uk
www.calclosets.co.uk

Cargo Homeshop
Tel: 01844 261 800

Chair Maker
54 Western Rd, Hove,
E Sussex BN3 1JD
Tel: 01273 777 810
email:
info@chairmaker.co.uk
www.chairmaker.co.uk

Chase Erwin
Tel: 020 7795 0555/7271
www.chase-erwin.com

Classic Choice
Tel: 0800 092 7711

Connections Interiors Ltd
286-288 Leigh Rd,
Leigh-on-Sea
Essex SS9 1BW
Tel: 01702 470 939
www.ccif.co.uk

David Jones Furniture Makers
Tel: 020 8572 6666
www.davidjones.uk.com

DM Design
Tel: 020 8871 1617

Dutch Connection
Tel: 01204 848 844
www.dutchconnection.co.uk

European Design Centre Ltd
Tel: 020 7255 2524
www.edcplc.com

Furniture123
www.furniture123.co.uk

Habitat
Tel: 0845 601 0740
www.habitat.net

Hideaway Beds Ltd
Tel: 01752 511 111
www.hideaway.co.uk

Matthew Hilton
Tel: 020 7739 1869
www.scp.co.uk

Jali
Tel: 01227 831 710

C & G Joinery
www.cgjoinery.co.uk.

Kartel
Tel: 020 7284 4963

Laura Ashley
Tel: 0870 562 2116
www.lauraashley.com

Lloyd Loom of Spalding
Tel: 01775 712 111
e-mail:
info@lloydloom.com
www.lloydloom.com

The London Bedding Company
Tel: 0800 783 3833
www.furniturevillage.co.uk

Megachoice
Tel: 020 8459 6969

Mondital
Tel: 020 8556 1221

Next
Tel: 0845 600 7000
www.next.co.uk

Northampton Signs
Tel: 01604 758 198

Ottima (S. J. & F. Ltd)
Tel: 01273 430 964
www.ottima.co.uk

Pearce Pebody
Tel: 01604 401 201
www.pearcepebody.com

Protocol furniture
Tel: 020 8591 6770
www.protocoluk.com

Purves and Purves
80-83 Tottenham Court Rd
London W1P 9HD
Tel: 020 7580 8223

Radwell
Tel: 01280 841 212

Reproduction furniture
Tel: 01935 706 331
www.reproductionfurniture.
com

RgcA
Montspur House,
22 Little Church St, Rugby,
Warks CV21 3AW
Tel: 01788 569 945

Richard Henry
Furnishings
Tel: 01274 653 057
for stockists
www.richardhenry.net

Scumble Goosie
Tel: 01453 731 305
www.scumble-goosie.co.uk

Sharps
Tel: 0800 789 789
www.sharps.co.uk

Sofa City Upholstery
Tel: 020 7254 8385

Thomas Stoddart Ltd
Tel: 0800 092 1456
www.thomas-stoddart.co.uk

Stonebridge Joinery
Works Ltd
Tel: 020 8965 5041
www.seating4u.com

SwiftCure Group
Tel: 01322 441 144
www.swiftcure.co.uk

Verdigris
Tel: 020 7703 8373

Vitra
Tel: 020 7608 6200
www.vitra.com

Viva Sofa
Tel: 01443 239 444
www.vivasofa.co.uk

E. & A. Wates
Tel: 020 8769 2205

HEATING

Acova Radiators
(UK) Ltd
Tel: 01562 753 001
e-mail: sales@acovarads
.demon.co.uk

Bisque Radiators
Tel: 01225 469 244

C. J. Electrical
(Ipswich) Ltd
Tel: 01473 280 111
www.cjelectrical.co.uk

Hudevad Britain
Tel: 01932 247 835
e-mail: sales@hudevad.co.uk

Internal Climate
Control Ltd
Tel: 01483 537 000
www.heatprofile.co.uk

Making Metal Work Ltd
Gerddu Bach Talog
Camarthenshire SA33 6PF
Tel: 01994 448 470

Myson
Tel: 0191 491 7500
www.myson.co.uk

Radiating Style
Tel: 020 8577 9111
www.radiatingstyle.co.uk

Vasco UK Ltd
Tel: 01933 278 802

Warmup Plc
Tel: 020 8992 9500
www.warmup.co.uk

Worcester Heat
Systems Ltd
Cotswold Way, Warndon
Worcester WR4 9SW
Tel: 01905 754 624

Jali
Tel: 01227 831 710
e-mail: sales@jali.co.uk
www.jali.co.uk

Taskworthy
Tel: 01873 821 430
e-mail:
enquiries@taskworthy.co.uk
www.taskworthy.co.uk

Fires

B&D Design
Tel: 020 7289 0545

Burlington Slate Ltd
Tel: 020 7976 7676

Corinthian Fireplaces
54 Charlton Rd
Shepton Mallet BA4 5PB
Tel: 01749 330 590

CVO Fire
Tel: 020 7580 5333
www.cvofirevault.co.uk

Fireplace World
Tel: 020 8406 1001

National Fireplace
Association
6th Floor,
The McLaren Building
35 Dale End, Birmingham
B4 7LN

Platonic Fireplace
Company
Tel: 020 8891 5904
www.platonicfireplaces.co.uk

Real Flame
Tel: 020 7731 5025
e- mail:
info@realflame.co.uk.

Red
Arch 4, Culvert Place,
Battersea,
London SW11 5BA
Tel: 020 7622 2221
e-mail: crafts@hotmail.com
www.redmetal.co.uk

Stone Productions Ltd
Tel: 020 8871 9257

TipTop Trading
Tel: 01895 258 222

KITCHEN DESIGN

Doors of Distinction
Tel: 020 8309 6400

Febo Designs
Tel: 01730 825 041

Integra Interiors Ltd
Tel: 0800 097 7377
www.integra-interiors.com

Andrew Macintosh
Furniture
462-464 Chiswick High Rd
London W4 5TT
Tel: 020 8995 8333

Niche Interiors and
Design House
Niche Interiors, 4 Artizan Rd
Northants NN1 4HU
Tel: 01604 601 609

Select Design Interiors
Tel: 020 8462 5608
e-mail: sdiuk@hotmail.com

KITCHEN UNITS

Richard Donkersley
Tel: 01458 441 122

Premier Sheet Metals
Tel: 023 9247 2633

Saffrey's Furniture
Tel: 01730 829 744
e-mail: saffroys@oxcitc.co.uk

Ultima Furniture
Systems Ltd
Langthwaite Grange
Industrial Park, South
Kerby WS9 3NR
Tel: 01977 608 608

Butterfields
Selbourne Road
Luton, Bedfordshire LU4 8QF
Tel: 01582 491 133

Promart
Unit 2B Knowsley Ind
Estate, Prescott,
Merseyside L34 9HP
Tel: 0151 547 4666

Pyrolave UK
Tel: 01428 707 154
www.pyrolave.com

Smarta Systems
5 The Courtyard, D'arcy
Business Park, South
Wales SA10 6EJ
Tel: 01792 818184
www.smartasystems.co.uk

Avilion Ltd
Orwell Close, Fairview
Industrial Park, Rainham,
Essex RM13 8UB
Tel: 01708 526 361

De Dietrich
Tel: 0870 750 3503
www.brandt.com/uk

Design Matters
Tel: 01628 531 584
www.dmkbb.co.uk

Glen Dimplex Heating
Tel: 0870 727 0101
www.glendimplex.com

Supply, British
Gypsum
www.british-
gypsum.bpb.com

Polyray UK Ltd
Tel: 020 8951 6300
www.polyray.com

Prentice Kitchens
Tel: 01827 287 387
www.prenticefurniture.com

LIGHTING

Abbey Lighting
Tel: 01789 400 705
www.abbeylighting.co.uk

Albion Court Ltd
Idea Works, New Rd
Gillingham SP8 4JH
Tel: 01747 822 818

Ann's of Kensington
Tel: 020 7937 5033

Architrade
Tel: 01535 681 284

Arriba Nova
Brilliant Lighting
Tel: 020 8898 3131

Artemide
Tel: 020 7631 5200
www.artemide.com

B&Q Warehouse
Tel: 0845 309 3099

Better Lighting
Tel: 01536 415 138

Columbia Glassworks
Tel: 020 7613 5155
info@columbia-
glass.co.uk

C. R. S. Electrical
Wholesalers Ltd
Tel: 020 7924 0377
www.crs-electrical.com

CTO Lighting Ltd
35 Park Avenue North
London N8 7RU
Tel: 020 8340 4593

Dar lighting
Tel: 01295 259 391

Design 4 Lighting
Tel: 020 8342 0994/5
www.design4lighting.co.uk

Environmental
Lighting Ltd
74-75 Barton Rd, Eccles,
Manchester M30 7AE
Tel: 0161 789 8686

Eyecube
Tel: 020 8743 1566

Hamilton Litestat Group
Tel: 01747 860 088
www.hamilton-litestat.com

IBL
Tel: 020 8391 5252
e-mail: info@ibl.co.uk
www.ibl.co.uk

iGuzzini
www.iguzzini.co.uk

IKEA
www.ikea.co.uk

Jali Lifestyle
Tel: 01227 831 710
www.jali.co.uk

John Lewis
Tel: 020 7629 7711

LED Group
Tel: 00 353 1 455 0770
www.led.ie

Lightform Ltd
Tel: 020 8778 2422

Mathmos
Tel: 020 7549 2700

Max Watt Design
Tibenham, Norfolk
Tel: 01379 674 440

Micromark
Tel: 020 8829 6354
www.micromark.co.uk

MK Electrics Ltd
Tel: 01268 563 000
www.mkelectrics.co.uk

Neptune Shades
Tel: 01304 362 397
www.neptuneshades.com

Optime Lighting
Tel: 01462 441 920
www.optime1.co.uk

Pearl Dot Ltd
Tel: 020 7609 3169
www.pearldot.com

SLI Lighting Ltd
Tel: 01273 616 647
Available at selected B&Q
stores

The Wholesale
Lighting Company
Tel: 020 7278 8993
e-mail: Sales
@wholesalelighting.co.uk

Christopher Wray
Lighting
Tel: 020 7751 8701
www.christopher-wray.com

MISCELLANEOUS

Alessi
Tel: 020 7491 2428

All Frames (UK) Ltd
Tel: 020 8676 8833
www.Allframes.co.uk

Aria
Tel: 020 7704 1999
www.ariashop.co.uk

Artefact
Tel: 020 7580 4878
e-mail:
artefactlondon@talk21.com

Bath Aqua Glass
Tel: 01225 428 146
www.bathaquaglass.com

Blue Mango
www.blue-mango.co.uk

Giles Blunden
Tel: 07740 466 092
www.eyecube.co.uk

Britannia Mirrors
Tel: 020 8985 2787
www.britanniamirrors.co.uk

Mimi Bromberg Ltd
Tel: 07930 443 488
www.mimibromberg.com

Bryony Burn
Flat 3, 241 Dickenson Rd,
Manchester M13 0YW
Tel: 0161 429 7778
Available at The Conran
Shop

David Robert Carter
Architectural Blacksmith,
Wisbech St Mary PE13 4SE
Tel: 01945 410 547

Shakir Chaker
422e The Custard Factory,
Gibb St, Birmingham
B9 4AA
Tel: 0121 693 0199

The Conran Shop
81 Fulham Rd, London
SW3 6RD
Tel: 020 7589 7401

Cookcraft.com
Tel: 01922 416 555
e-mail:
info@cookcraft.com
www.cookcraft.com

Christian Day Ltd
Tel: 01299 250 385
www.potsandplanters.co.uk

Divertimenti
139-141 Fulham Rd,
London SW3 6SD
Tel: 020 7581 8065
e-mail:
fulham@divertimenti.co.uk

Dorma
PO Box 7, Lees St, Swinton,
Manchester M27 6DB
Tel: 0161 251 4400

S. & B. Evans & Sons
Tel: 020 7729 6635
e-mail:
evans@thecitygardenpottery
.co.uk

Fairfield Displays
Tel: 01252 812 211

Elephant Ltd
Tel: 020 7637 7930

Fearless
11 Fore St, Port Isaac
Tel: 01208 880 297

Framework Picture
Framing
Tel: 020 8691 5140

Anna French
343 King's Rd,
London SW3 5ES
Tel: 020 7351 1126

The Gallery
on the Green
18 The Links,
Concord Centre,
London W12 8PP
Tel: 020 8749 7335

Glover And Smith
9a Winchester St,
Overton, nr. Basingstoke,
Hants RG25 3HR
Tel: 01256 773 012
e-mail:
sales@gloverandsmith.com
www.gloverandsmith.com

The Gothic Revival
Tel: 01484 646 924
www.mywebpage.net/gothic.
revival

Rolf C. Hagen
Tel: 01977 556 622
www.hagen.com

The KM Harris Tweed
Group
Rae MacKenzie
Tel: 01851 702 772

Heals
Tottenham Court Rd,
London W1
Tel: 020 7896 7546

The Holding Company
241-245 Kings Rd,
London SW3 5FI
Tel: 020 7352 1600
e-mail:
mail@theholdingcompany.
co.uk

Jerry's Homestore
Tel: 020 7581 0909

Kitschen Synch
Tel: 020 7497 5129

Liberty Plc
Regent St,
London W1R 6AH
Tel: 020 7734 1234

Loco Glass
Tel: 0870 606 1290
www.locoglass.co.uk

Loomer
Tel: 0113 226 0685
www.thunderstrand.com

Modern Home
Comforts
Tel: 0800 052 6398

Andrew Muirhead
and Son Ltd
Tel: 0141 554 3724
www.muirhead.co.uk

Annette Naudin Studio
108F The Big Peg,
120 Vyse St,
Birmingham B18 6NF
Tel: 0121 248 2428

Overdose on Design
182 Brick Lane, London E1
Tel: 020 7613 1266

The Pine Corner
272–274 Lewisham High St,
London SE13
Tel: 020 8690 4620

Pivotelli
Tel: 01481 246 818
www.pivotelli.co.uk

The Precision Plastic
Ball Co Ltd
Tel: 01943 831 166
www.theppb.co.uk

Prima
Tel: 0113 251 1500

Putsch ltd
Unit 1 Hurst Barns,
Hurst Lane
Privett, Nr Alton,
Hants GU34 3PL
Tel: 01730 825 041

Retro Home
20 Pembridge Rd,
London W11
Tel: 020 7221 2055

Roberts Radio
Tel: 01709 571 722

The Rock Shop
Tel: 01484 485 109
sales@burhouse.demon.co.uk

The Shed
Tel: 07977 585 948

STP- Group Limited
Watford Bridge Works,
New Mills,
High Peak SK22 4HJ
Tel: 01663 744 030

Tree Works
13 Woodfield Rd, Ealing,
London W5 1SL
Tel: 020 8537 2896

Village Glass
Tel: 01376 503 838

Nick and Gabi Ward
18-24 Westbourne Grove,
London W2 5RH
Tel: 020 7243 0203

Waterford Crystal Ltd
Tel: 00 353 5 137 3311

Webbs Furniture
www.webbsfurniture.co.uk

Wheredidyoubuythat
.com
Tel: 0191 482 3444
www.wheredidyoubuythat
.com

White and Gray
113c Northcote Rd,
London SW11 6PW
Tel: 020 7787 8173

Matthew Lloyd-
Winderís
104 Myddleton Rd,
Bowes Park
London N22 4NQ
Tel: 020 8889 5782

PAINT

Armourcoat Ltd
Tel: 01732 460 668
www.armourcoat.co.uk

Blackfriar Ltd
Tel: 01275 854 911
www.blackfriar.co.uk

Designers Guild
Tel: 020 7243 7300
www.designersguild.com

Hammerite Products Ltd
Tel: 01661 830 000
www.hammerite.com

Ray Munn Ltd
861-863 Fulham Rd
London SW6 5HP
Tel: 020 7736 9876
www.raymunn.com

Paintworks
Tel: 020 7792 8012
www.paintworks.co.uk

Southern Coatings
Tel: 020 8644 6670

W. Habberley
Meadows
Tel: 0121 770 0103
www.habberleymeadows
.co.uk.

Rian Kanduth
Tel: 07855 981 199
kanduthrian@hotmail.com

PLASTERWORK

Plaster Alabaster
Tel: 020 8441 2677
plastala@hotmail.com

Plaster Effects
Tel: 020 8577 2090

Star Motifs
Tel: 07887 887 017

PLUMBING

A. W. Andes
Tel: 01920 404 040
for stockists

Franke UK Ltd
Tel 0161 436 6280
www.franke.co.uk

PlumbFast
Tel: 0800 026 5454

Waterline Ltd
Tel: 0870 556 1560

SCULPTURE AND ARTWORK

Colourlink
Tel: 020 7549 8231
www.goodspeed.co.uk

Andy Goldsworthy prints
www.eyestorm.com

Hamar Acrylic
Tel: 020 7739 2907

Paul Kessling
Iel: 01235 862 513
e-mail: Paul.Kessling
@btinternet.com

Paul Lewis Sculptures
Units 7 & 8, Riverway
Industrial Estate, Isle of
Wight, PO30 5UX
Tel: 01983 524 573

Shoosmith
Tel: 07855 026 457

SPECIALIST DECORATION

Abingdon Stone and
Marble Ltd
Tel: 01235 520 617
www.abingdon-stone.co.uk

Rags Decorating
Consultants
Tel: 01737 357 330

Round Green
Engineering
Tel: 01582 503 808

TILES

Amabis Handmade
Tiles Ltd
Ubique Park, March Way,
Shrewsbury, Salop SY1 3JE
Tel: 01743 461 700
www.amabis.co.uk

The Ashbourne Brick
and Tile Company Ltd
Tel: 01335 342 809

Coral Ceramics
Tel: 01782 212861
email:
lawrence@coralceramics.
freeserve.co.uk

Landford Stone
Tel: 01794 324 232

Pilkington Tiles
Tel: 0161 727 1111

Reid Harris
Tel: 020 7736 7511
e-mail: architectural@
reid-harris.co.uk

Sculpta Ceramics
Tel: 01782 575 707
www.scuplta.co.uk.

Mr Tim Sorrellas
Tel: 023 8086 6344
e-mail: Sorrellas@
cw.com.net

The Tile Association
Freephone 0800 783 8886

The Tile Gallery
Tel: 020 7385 8818

Exteriors

BLINDS

Conservatory Blinds
Ltd
PO Box 767, Morden,
Surrey SM4 6SW
Tel: 0800 071 8888
e-mail: info@conservatory
blinds.co.uk
www.conservatoryblinds.co.uk

Luxaflex
Tel: 0800 039 9399
for stockists
www.luxaflex.com

BUILDING MATERIALS

A. B. G. Construction Ltd
Tel: 020 8440 3568

Alpha Pneumatic
Supplies Ltd
Unit 5a Abbey Industrial
Estate, Mitcham, Surrey
CR4 4NA
Tel: 020 8687 0411

Bespoke Precast Ltd
Weltharne Lane,
Ingbirch, Worth,
Penistone,
Sheffield S36 7GJ
Tel: 01226 761 000

J. W. Bollom & Co Ltd
Tel: 020 8658 2299

Camfaud Concrete
Pumps Ltd
High Rd, Thornwood
Common, Epping,
Essex CM16 6LU
Tel: 01992 560 898

A.W. Champion Ltd
Champion House,
Burlington Rd, New
Malden, Surrey KT3 4NB
Tel: 020 8949 1621
for stockists

Compass Plumbing
and Heating
Units 2-4 Stirling
Industrial Estate,
Essex RM10 8CX
Tel: 020 8595 3143

Jon English
Developments Ltd
4 Wasdale Close, Halfway,
Sheffield S20 4HA
Tel: 0114 248 0786

Fleet Minimix
The Old Sun Wharf,
Crete Hall Rd
North Fleet, Kent DA11 9AA
Tel: 01474 357 632

Jewsons
Tel: 0800 539 766 for
stockists

Marshalls Brier Lodge
Southowram, Halifax,
W Yorkshire HX3 9SY
Tel: 0870 120 7474 for
brochure
www.marshalls.co.uk

Morgan Timber
Knight Rd, Rochester
Kent ME2 2BA
Tel: 01634 290 909
e-mail:
info@morgantimber.co.uk
www.morgantimber.co.uk

Norcros Adhesives Ltd
Longton Rd, Trentham,
Stoke-on-Trent ST4 8JB
Tel: 01782 591 100

PCI Construction
Systems Ltd
Tel: 0191 428 2266
www.pci-construction-
systems.co.uk

Processing &
Merchanting UK
Prescot Rd, St Helen's
WA10 3TT
Tel. 01744 692 000

Ramcrete Pumping
Services Ltd
14 Bray Rd, Berkshire SL6
Tel: 01628 782 860

RMC Readymix Ltd
Head Office, Crown House,
Rugby, Warks CV21 2DT
Tel: 01932 568 833
Information: 0800 667 827
e-mail:
info.readmix@rmc.co.uk
www.rmc.co.uk

Smith & Sons Quarry
Tel: 01869 331 281

Stephenson
Construction
The Barn, Petworth Rd,
Kirdford, W Sussex
RH14 0NL
Tel: 01403 820 691

Thermalite
Marley Building Materials,
Station Rd, Birmingham
B46 1HP
Tel: 01675 468 429
e-mail: thermalite@mbm-
marley.co.uk
www.thermalite.co.uk

Travis Perkins
Tel: 0870 500 5500 for
stockists

Trueform Ltd
78 Suez Rd, Brimsdown,
Enfield, Middlesex EN3 7PS
Tel: 020 8805 7335
www.trueformltd.co.uk

Walkers – The
Builders Merchant
Cray Ave, Orpington
B25 3RX
Tel: 01689 822 785
www.walkersbm.fsnet.co.uk

London Road
West Thurrock, Grays
Essex RM20 3LU
Tel: 01708 867 237

ELECTRICAL

Event Security
Systems Ltd
Barnoast, Woodfalls
Industrial Estate, Kent
ME18 6DA
Tel: 01622 871 116

JBL Arbiter Pro Audio
Tel. 020 8202 1199
www.arbitergroup.com

Optikenetics Ltd
38 Cromwell Rd,
Luton LU3 1DN
Tel: 01582 411 413
www.optikinetics.com

Skears Photographic
76 Baliff St,
Northampton NN1 3DZ
Tel: 01604 630 675
e-mail: sales@skears-
photographic.co.uk

Supracables
Unit 7, Wren Industrial
Estate, Coldred Rd,
Kent ME15 9YT
Tel: 01622 664 070
www.supracables.co.uk

Tannoy Ltd
Coatbridge, Strathclyde
ML5 4TF
Tel: 01236 420 199
www.tannoy.com

FURNITURE

Arbor Vetum
The Brickyards, Steep
Marsh, Petersfield,
Hampshire GU32 2BN
Tel: 01730 893 000
e-mail:
info@arbovetum.co.uk
www.arborvetum.co.uk

Cider House Furniture
Tel: 01395 443 111
www.ciderhouse.co.uk

Dillons
Garden Sheds Ltd
Old Redbridge Rd,
Redbridge, Southampton,
Hants SO15 0AN
Tel: 023 8087 3787

Spencer Fung's
Architects
Tel: 020 8960 9883

Furniture Frontiers
37-39 Pembridge Rd,
Notting Hill,
London W11 3HG
Tel: 020 7727 6132

Gardens and Beyond
47 Highgate High St,
London N6 5JX
Iel: 020 8445 6446
www.gardensbeyond.com

Lister Lutyens
Company Ltd
Hammonds Drive,
Eastborne
E Sussex BN23 6PW
Tel: 01323 431 177
email: saleatlister-
lutyens.co.uk
www.lister-lutyens.co.uk

Oxley's Furniture
Tel: 01386 840 466
www.oxleys.com

Premier Sheds
Streatham Common,
Station Approach, London
SW16 5NR
Tel: 020 8677 0459
www.shedandfencing.co.uk

Rowlinson Garden
Tel: 01270 506 900

Willy Guhl
TwentyTwentyOne, London
Tel: 020 7288 1996
www.twentytwentyone.com

GLASS

Barretts Glass & Glazing
Unit 19, 87 Crampton St,
London SE17 3AZ
Tel: 020 7252 7876

Juno Glass Ltd
46–50 Lydden Rd,
London SW18 4LR
Tel: 020 8870 9293
Freephone 0800 279 4527
www.junoglass.co.uk

J. Preedy & Son Ltd
Lamb Works, London N7
9DP
Tel: 020 7700 0377

Stevenage Glass
Tel: 0800 146 311

HEATING

Bisque Radiators
Tel: 020 7328 2225
e-mail: Info@bisquelondon
.demon.co.uk

Clifton Nurseries
Tel: 020 7289 6851

Nipoori UK Ltd
85b Main Rd, Romford,
Essex RM2 5EL
Tel: 01708 729 123
e-mail: sales@nipooria.com
www.nipooria.com

The Outdoor Deck Company
Mortimer House, 46 Sheen
Lane, London SW14 8LP
e-mail:
www.outdoordeck.co.uk

Petts Wood Energy Centre
172 Pettswood Rd, Kent
BR5 ILS
Tel: 01689 890 028

Sovereign Distribution (UK) Ltd
Sovereign House, 34
Robeson Way,
Hertfordshire WD6 5RY
Tel: 02083 865 122
e-mail:
sales@fiesta-heater.com

Morso Stoves
Tel: 0121 386 6306
www.morsostoves.co.uk

Xceptional Designs
Tel: 01469 530 992
www.xdes.co.uk

HIRE TOOLS

Bywaters Waste and Recycling Management
Auckland Rd, Leyton,
London E10 5NB
Tel: 020 8558 1141

Caterpillar (UK) Ltd
www.cat.com

Finning (UK) Ltd
Tel: 01543 461 461
e-mail:
Mailbox@finning.co.uk

H. E. Services Ltd
Tel: 01634 291 290

Plant and Tool hire
11-15 Abbeybard Rd
High Wickham, Bucks
HP11 1RS
Tel: 01494 450 389

Speedy Hire Centre
For nearest centre call:
Midlands – 01332 380 493
Northern – 01744 697 000
Southern – 01284 760 842

Takeuchi MFG (UK) Ltd
Lynch Plant Hire, Fourth
Way, Wembley, Middlesex
HA9 OLH
Tel: 01706 657 722
e-mail:
sales@takeuchi-mfg.co.uk
www.takeuchi-mfg.co.uk

LIGHTING

AC/DC Lighting Systems Ltd
Pasture Lane Works,
Barrowford, Nelson,
Lancashire BB9 6ES
Tel: 01282 601 464

AICO Ltd
Mile End Business Park
Shropshire SY10 8NN
Tel: 01691 657 466
www.aico.co.uk

Artemide
106 Great Russell St
London WC1B 3NB
Tel: 020 7631 5200
e-mail: Info@artemide.co.uk
www.artemide.com

Creative Garden Lighting
18 Hopton Close, Daventry,
Northamptonshire
NN11 5GF
Freephone: 0800 068 0548
www.gardenlight.co.uk

Evergreen Electrical
Tel: 020 8309 7722
www.evergreenelectrical
.co.uk

Lighting for Gardens
Tel: 01462 817 000
www.lightingforgardens.com

Range Electrical Supplies
12 Salisbury Rd, Bromley
Kent BR2
Tel: 0208 290 6028

Ring Lighting
Gelderd Rd,
Leeds LS12 6NB
Stockists through B&Q only

Ryness
Tel: 020 7278 8993
for stockists
www.ryness.co.uk

Schott Fibre Optics (UK) Ltd
Shaw Lane Industrial
Estate, Ogden Rd,
Doncaster DN2 4SQ
Tel: 01302 361 574
e-mail:
enquiries@schott.co.uk
www.schott-fibreoptics.com

Solopark Plc
Tel: 01223 834 663
www.solopark.co.uk

Sugg Lighting Ltd
Tel: 01293 540 111
www.sugglighting.co.uk

Thorn Lighting
Tel: 01708 766 033
www.thornlight.com

West London Security
19 Stannary St
London SE11 4AA
Tel: 0800 328 1971
www.westlondonsecurity.com

The Wholesale Lighting & Electrical Company
Tel: 020 7278 8993
www.wholesalelighting.co.uk

METAL

A4 Plus Drawing Services Ltd
Fenview Lodge, Doddington,
Cambs PE15 0SN
Tel: 01354 742 000
e-mail:
enquiries@a4plus.co.uk
www.a4plus.co.uk

Avesta Polarit Stainless
Tel: 0114 261 4591

Brandon Steels
799 London Rd, West
Thurrock, Essex RM20 3LH
Tel: 01708 864 028

Calmel's Design & Construction Ltd
3-5-7 Southville, Wandsworth
Rd, London SW8 2PR
Tel: 020 7622 6181
www.calmels.co.uk

CAMTRACK
Unit 6, Highbury, Brandon,
Surrey IP27 OND
Tel: 01842 811 111

Craufurd Engineering
135b Edinburgh Ave
Trading Estate, Slough SL1
4SW
Tel: 01753 531 462
e-mail: administrator
@craufurd.com

'The Cutting Edge' Group Ltd
Sun St, Sawbridgeworth,
Hertfordshire CM21 9PU
Tel: 01279 306 306
e-mail:
sales@thecuttingedge.co.uk
www.thecuttingedge.co.uk

C. Downhills
Unit D, Riverside Way,
Uxbridge UB8 2YS
Tel: 01895 813 150

Elite Metalcraft
Tel: 020 8810 5122
www.elitemetalcraft.co.uk

Stewart Fraser Ltd
Henwood Industrial Estate,
Ashford, Kent TN24 8DR
Tel: 01233 625 911

James Hunt
Tel: 0800 389 4974
www.jhrnr.co.uk

Industrial Metal Services
Tel: 01753 681 222

Integrated Metal Solutions
17b Bakers Court, Paycocke
Rd, Basildon, Essex
Tel: 01268 534 133
www.integratedmetalsolutions
.com

Maccaferri Environmental Solutions
7400 The Quorum, North
Garsington Rd,
Oxford OX4 2JZ
Tel: 01865 770 555

The Regent Street Wrought Iron Works
180-186 Regent St,
Kettering,
Tel: 01536 485 892

RS Components Ltd
Tel: 01536 405 161
http://rswww.com

Sixsmiths Ltd
Workshop: Arch 11,
Culvert Place, Battersea,
London SW11 5BA
Tel: 020 7498 2977
e-mail:
sixsmiths@clara.net
www.sixsmiths.clara.net

C.F. Sparrowhawk Ltd
24 Epsom Lane, Tadworth,
Surrey KT20 5EH
Tel: 01737 352 889

Tip Top Trading
Tel: 01895 258 222
www.tiptopalloys.co.uk

MISCELLANEOUS

The Amtico Company
Tel: 024 7686 1400

Arch Way Ceramics
Peter Barn Gallery,
Beckhouse, South
Amberhoam, W Sussex
Tel: 01798 861 3888

D+S Tarpaulins
Evergreen, Groves Rd,
Eastchurch, Sheerness,
Kent ME12 3SY
Tel: 01795 880 956

Ells and Farrier
20 Beak St,
London W1R 3HA
Tel: 020 7629 9964

Forsham Cottage Ark
Tel: 01233 820 229
www.forshamcottagearks.co
.uk

Innovations McCord
Tel: 0870 908 7005
www.emccord.com

Jali
Tel: 01227 831 710

Jazz-Art-Deco
27 St Peters Ave,
Haslingden, Rossendale,
Lancashire BB4 4BS

Mathmos
179 Drury Lane,
London WC2
Tel: 020 7549 2743

John Old
9 Stratford Rd, London W8
Tel: 020 7565 8808
www.jonold.co.uk

Oxford Architectural
Tel: 01367 242 268
e-mail:
feedback@oxfordarchitectur
al.co.uk

Pots and Pithoi
The Barns, East St,
Turners Hill
W Sussex RH10 4QQ
Tel: 01342 714 793
www.pots-and-pithoi.co.uk

Tall Ships Playframes
Tel: 01840 212 022
www.tallships.co.uk

TP Activity Toys Ltd
Tel: 01299 872 800
e-mail: customerservices
@tptoys.com

PAVING

**Albion Stone
Quarries Ltd**
27-33 Brighton Rd
Redhill, Surrey RH1 6PP
Tel: 01737 771 772
www.albionstonequarries
.com

County Wide Paving
14 Glenluce Rd, London
SE3 7SB
Tel: 0800 015 5165

Hornton Masonry Co.
Edge Hill, Oxfordshire
OX15 6DX
Tel: 01295 670 238
or 01295 670 570

Marshalls Clay Cobble
Brier Lodge,
W Yorkshire HX3 9SY
Tel: 0870 120 7474
for stockists
Tel: 01422 306 300
for advice
www.marshalls.co.uk

Quiligotti Ltd
Tel: 0161 727 1000

Stanley's Quarry
Upton Wold,
Morton-in-Marsh,
Gloucestershire GL56 9TR
Tel: 01386 841 236
www.cotswoldstone.com

Stonemarket Ltd
Oxford Rd, Ryton-on-
Dunsmore,
Warwickshire CV8 3EJ
Tel: 024 7651 8700
www.stonemarket.co.uk

J. Suttle
Swanage Quarries
Tel: 01929 423 576
www.stone.uk.com

Walshs Reclaimed
Tel: 0161 789 8223
e-mail: walshs@
manchester.fsnet.co.uk

Yorkdale Natural Ltd
Old Kingston Rd, Worcester
Park, Surrey KT4 7QH
Tel: 020 8337 9922

PAINT

Dulux
Tel: 01753 550 555

Ray Munn
Tel: 020 7736 9876
www.raymunn.co.uk

Outside White
Geedon Ltd, Whitehall Rd,
Colchester, Essex CO2 8HX
Tel: 01206 797 556

**Plasti–Kote Spray
Paints**
Tel: 01223 836 400

Weber Shandwick
Tel: 020 7950 2814

PLANTS

Anglo Aquatic Plants
Tel: 020 8363 8548

Architectural Plants
Tel: 01403 891 772
www.architecturalplants.com

Ausferns
Cow-watering Lane,
Writtle, Chelmsford, Essex
Tel: 01245 421 999
Tel (mail order):
01245 359 433
e-mail:
Ausfer@globalnet.co.uk

Belwood Trees
Brigton of Ruthven, Meigle,
Perthshire PH12 8RQ
Tel: 01828 640 219
e-mail:
belwood.trees@virgin.net
www.belwoodtrees.co.uk

Civic Tree Care Ltd
Forestry House, PO Box 23,
Tring, Herts HP23 4AE
Tel: 01442 825 401
e-mail: info@civictrees.co.uk
www.civictrees.co.uk

Iden Croft Herbs
Frittenden Rd,
Kent TN12 0DH
Tel: 01580 891 432
e-mail: idencroft.herbs
@dial.pipex.com

Kingley Plant Centre
Sedge Green,
Essex EN9 2PA
Tel: 01992 465 073

**Pantiles Plant
& Garden Centre**
Almners Rd,
Surrey KT16 0BJ
Tel: 01932 872 195

**Plants Waterers
Nurseries**
Bagshot, Surrey GU19 5DG
Tel: 01276 480 200

Tendercare
Southlands Rd, Denham,
Uxbridge, Middx UB9 4HD
Tel: 01895 835 544

**Woodcote Green
Nurseries**
Woodmansterne Land,
Surrey
Tel: 020 8647 6838

TILES

Pilkingtons UK Ltd
Tel: 0161 727 1000

'Rock Revelations'
1 Cransley Hill,
Northampton N14
Tel: 01536 791 737
e-mail: sales@rock-
revelations.co.uk
www.rockrevelations.co.uk

**Ruby Architectural
Services Ltd**
Unit 23/24, Cromwell
Industrial Estate, Staffa Rd,
London E10 7QZ
Tel: 020 8558 8399

**Smith and Wareham
Tile Merchants**
Eastgate St, Bury St.
Edmunds, Suffolk IP33 1YQ
Tel: 01284 704 188
www.smithandwareham
.co.uk

Specifications Ltd
Tel: 01270 886 214
e-mail:
sales@specltd.demon.co.uk

The Tile Association
Tel: 020 8663 0946

TIMBER

BSW Timber Plc
Holly House Estate,
Middlewich Rd, Cranage,
Cheshire CW10 9LT
Tel: 01606 839 100

Champions Timber
Tel: 020 8949 1621
www.championtimber.com

Crestala Fencing
South Farm, Kent TN3 9JN
Tel: 01892 864 646

Howath Timber
Lincoln Castle, Lincoln
Castle Way, Lincolnshire
DN19 SRR
Tel: 01469 532 300

LASSCO Flooring
41 Maltby St,
London SE1 3PA
Tel: 020 7237 4488
e-mail:
flooring@lassco.co.uk
www.lassco.co.uk

**Lawsons Timber &
Fencing**
1208 High Rd,
London N20 0LL
Tel: 020 8446 1321
e-mail:
lawsons@zipmail.co.uk

Oak Lower Farm
Brandon Lane,
Coventry CV3 3GW
Tel: 02476 639 338

**Timber Decking
Association**
PO Box 99, A1 Business
Park, Pontefract,
W Yorkshire WF11 0YY
Tel: 01977 679 812
www.tda.org.uk

Timeless Timber
BSW Timber Plc,
Middlewich Rd,
Cheshire CW10 9LT
Tel: 01606 839 100

Woodside Timber
Tel: 020 8654 1256

TURF & TOPSOIL

J. Arthur Bower's
Firth Rd, Lincoln LN6 7AH
Tel: 01522 537 561

**E.A. Goundry & Son
Ltd**
Duns Tew, Oxon OX6 4JR
Tel: 01869 340 224

**The London
Lawn Turf Company**
Elm Rd, Surrey SM6 7HF
Tel: 0800 028 6059
www.londonlawnturf.co.uk

**Charles Morris
Fertilizers**
Longford House,
Long Lane, Stanwell,
Middlesex TW19 7AT
Tel: 01784 449 144
e-mail: charlesmorris
@btinternet.com

Rolawn
Tel: 01904 608 661
e-mail: info@rolawn-
turf.co.uk
www.rolawn.co.uk

**Thompsons Plant &
Garden Centre**
Tel: 020 8302 2455

Town and Country Turf
Tel: 01322 666 707

WATER

**The Creek Aquatic
Garden Centre**
Thames Valley KOI, 427
Walton Rd, West Molesey,
Surrey KT8 2EJ
Tel: 020 8941 8758
www.koicarpuk.co.uk

David Curtis & Son
Tel: 01322 666 814

Stewart Fraser Ltd
Henwood Industrial Estate,
Ashford, Kent TN24 8DR
Tel: 01233 625 911

Hozelock Ltd
Haddenham,
Bucks HP17 8JD
Tel: 01844 292 002
e-mail: consumer.services
@hozelock.com

**Landscape Watering
Systems**
Bratch Lane,
Wiltshire SP3 5EB
Tel: 01722 716 969
www.lws.uk.com

OASE (UK) Ltd
OASE House, 2 North Way,
Andover, Hants SP10 5AZ
Tel: 01264 333 225
Brochure: 0800 838 401
www.oase-uk.co.uk

Obart Pumps Ltd
Unit 1, Pattenden Lane,
Marden, Kent TN12 NQS
Tel: 0800 092 4423
www.obartpumps.co.uk

Soft Surfaces Ltd
1 Milwood Close, Cheadle,
Hulme, Cheshire SK8 6SU
Tel: 0161 485 4467

**South East
Galvanizers Ltd**
Tel: 01376 501 501

**Whitecross Rubber
Products Ltd**
Nazeing New Rd,
Herts EN10 6SX
Tel: 01992 467 053
www.ponds.co.uk

INDEX

This book is published to accompany the television series **Home Front**, which is produced by the BBC.

Series Producer: Amanda de Ryk

Published by BBC Worldwide Ltd,
Woodlands, 80 Wood Lane, London W12 0TT

First published 2001
Reprinted 2002
This paperback edition published 2002

ISBN: 0 563 48851 4

Commissioning Editor: Nicky Copeland
Project Editor: Helena Caldon
Book Design: Paul Vater at sugarfreedesign.co.uk
Cover Art Direction: Pene Parker
Picture Researcher: Bea Thomas
Photography: Robin Matthews
Styling for Photography: Marcia Morgan
Production Controller: Kenneth McKay

Set in Adobe Caslon and Din Mittelschrift
Printed and bound in France by Imprimerie Pollina s.a. n° L87001
Cover printed by Imprimerie Pollina s.a.
Colour separations by Kestrel Digital Colour Ltd, Chelmsford, Essex